WHERE FAITH BEGINS

Where
Faith Begins

C. ELLIS NELSON

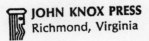

JOHN KNOX PRESS
Richmond, Virginia

Library of Congress Catalog Card Number: 67-22004
© M. E. Bratcher 1967
Printed in the United States of America
J. 4237

Dedicated to my mother
ELIZABETH STARK NELSON

Contents

The James Sprunt Lectures

Mr. James Sprunt of Wilmington, North Carolina, in 1911 established a perpetual lectureship at Union Theological Seminary in Virginia which would enable this institution to secure from time to time the services of distinguished ministers and authoritative scholars as special lecturers on subjects connected with various departments of Christian thought and Christian work. The lecturers are chosen by the faculty of the Seminary and a committee of the Board of Trustees, and the lectures are published after their delivery in accordance with a contract between the lecturer and these representatives of the institution.

The series of lectures on this Foundation for the year 1965 is presented in this volume.

Union Theological Seminary
in Virginia

Preface

Christians tend to think of the communication of religion in terms of the doctrines that should be explained, the agencies of communication (such as the Sunday school and youth groups), or the means of communication (such as preaching and teaching). This book deals with all of these elements of communication in an indirect way; but the main contention is that religion at its deepest levels is located within a person's sentiments and is the result of the way he was socialized by the adults who cared for him as a child. The vital question we need to answer is "How does a person develop trust in the God revealed to us in the Bible—particularly in Jesus Christ—and what does that faith mean in his life?"

To state the question that way moves us away from doctrines, agencies, and means of communication into questions such as the following: Why is there faith? How is faith transmitted? How is faith developed into meaning which can be communicated? Can such meaning be modified; if so, under what conditions? These and similar questions deal with presuppositions that underlie our religious outlook. Presuppositions are nonrational and cannot be verified or "proven"; yet our whole religious life is built on them. They give us our orientation, they provide the emotional support for the things to which we commit our life, and they supply the impulse that causes our mind to turn one way or another in search of satisfactory beliefs.

When we explore the nonrational basis of our religious life, we find ourselves in a territory where boundaries are not distinct. Religion blends into other aspects of personality, such as the quality and quantity of hope and the capacity to care for the welfare of other people. Moreover, the roots of our moral life—indeed, the desire to be a responsible person—are all intertwined in the soil that produces religious faith. Somewhere deep within a person's being are laid the presuppositions of faith. Our problem in this book is to describe how faith is communicated to a person and the way the church can use that process more deliberately and intelligently.

My thesis is that faith is communicated by a community of believers and that the meaning of faith is developed by its members out of their history, by their interaction with each other, and in relation to the events that take place in their lives.

There are two major questions that haunt any conceptual analysis of practical theology. The first is the relation of our modern empirical knowledge of man which comes from the social sciences to a Biblical description of man's nature. The second is an outgrowth of the first: Where is our authority or on what kind of evidence can we rely, now that historical-critical studies have eliminated a proof-text method of using the Bible. I do not claim to have given a definitive answer to either of these questions, but I believe I have been able to overcome their paralyzing effect.

My method is relatively easy to describe. It came to me, through my study of the historical-critical method and especially of form criticism, that before we can ask what the Bible says we have to ask *what it is*; then we have a way of analyzing what it says. The Bible is the book describing a community of people who by faith were able to discern God's message for them and to actualize his will in their lives. Thus, we have a collection of historical narratives, poems, war songs, drama, creeds, gospels, wisdom literature, parables, and prophecies. The reality with which we must deal is the communities that produced the Bible. As we read and study the literature these communities left us we must discover what their life was like, how they interpreted their past, and how they understood God's presence among them.

From my study of cultural anthropology and sociology, I discerned that what these social scientists were describing as the socializing process (or acculturation process) was the process by which faith and its meaning was transmitted by a community of believers. This occurred to me because I had begun to realize that culture deals with religious problems, such as the origin and destiny of the world and ethical codes of behavior; culture is also responsible for attitudes that are decisive in shaping a person's self-identity. This led me to see that the socializing process was a natural human phenomenon in Biblical times as well as today. Therefore by using the analytical methods of the social scientists who study human communities we could see how this process operated and use it for understanding and improving our communication of the Christian faith.

Although the method can be easily stated, its use for communicating our Christian faith is complex because the Christian faith claims a source of direction from outside culture. This means the Christian finds himself a product of culture, living in culture, and yet attempting to develop a way of life that is somewhat different from his culture. How the Christian can live this way cannot be answered precisely; but it is my conviction that we must raise the question and force tentative answers or religion will forever be at the mercy of the cultural value-system. Just to raise the question presents formidable problems. Many Christians have never attempted to analyze themselves in relation to the culture that produced them. This is, in part, because our unargued assumptions which come from culture are highly charged emotions; to examine them critically is a threatening experience we tend to avoid. In part, it is caused by the difficulty the average person has in understanding culture. Ralph Linton put it graphically in his comment that for a person to discover culture is like a fish discovering he is living in water. If the reader is not accustomed to self-examination in relation to the forces that formed him, he—like the fish—may be bewildered as to why so much is made of the obvious. But the "obvious" of culture is man-made, so it is the substance that has to be opened up for critical examination if faith in God is ever to lead us to a different style of life.

Culture, like a religious tradition, is historical. Therefore, this approach deals more with the matter of interpreting history than it does with systematic theology. The Bible is a series of recorded interpretations of tradition. Following that example, we have to interpret our past to fit the circumstances of today. But interpretation is a delicate matter. If we misunderstand our past, we lose guidance for today and we fail to know God as "the God of the living."

Such an analysis focuses attention on the present and on the future. This creates ambiguity. Our technology is developing so rapidly we hardly know what to expect in the near future except that we will gain more and more control over our environment, space, and biological functions. Each major technical advance has social implications. As we gain more control over life, the issues of how we shall use human life and the goals toward which we shall work become more acute. Technical advances also impinge on the practical everyday ethical decisions a person has to make, as illustrated by the change in sexual codes of behavior by reason of technical advances in birth control methods.

Thus, there is a terrible strain on conventional ethical codes, and the strain will become more severe in the future. The rate of social change is so rapid some observers say that conscience will no longer be the internal moral regulator in the future because it is always a generation behind the times. Although that statement is probably too radical, there is no question that conscience must be constantly refurbished to meet new conditions which were not in existence when conscience was formed in the present adult population a generation earlier. How will conscience be refurbished when one of the major characteristics of our emerging technical society is its lack of small face-to-face communities where life is shared, the meaning of life discussed, and the content of conscience determined?

I believe that the local church is the community that can develop a contemporary meaning of faith before it is passed on to the rising generation. This book is an attempt to show why this must be done, and the last chapter suggests ways it may be done. The proposals do not eliminate the Sunday school or any agency of instruction, but they suggest that we use them differently within the context of the congregation as the educator.

I want to express my appreciation of the Board of Trustees, the Faculty, and the late President Jas. A. Jones of Union Theological Seminary, Richmond, Virginia, for the invitation to give the James

Sprunt Lectures which occasioned the writing of this book. The hospitality Mrs. Nelson and I received during the Sprunt Lecture Week was so gracious and thoughtful that we shall remember it with pleasure the rest of our lives. I also appreciate the comments I received from ministers during the course of the lectures which helped me in revising this material for publication.

Before the lectures were given I was fortunate in having a sabbatical leave for one semester, which I spent in Mansfield College, Oxford University. Principal John Marsh kindly allowed me the privileges of the Senior Common Room. Thus, I had the benefit of stimulating conversation with Fellows of the University and the luxury of uninterrupted hours in the library. The trip to England and the freedom to pursue this line of inquiry were made possible by a faculty fellowship from the American Association of Theological Schools, for which I am profoundly grateful.

Several of my colleagues at Union Theological Seminary have given generously of their time and judgment in reading this book. James Louis Martyn, in reading most of the manuscript, has prevented me from making many errors of interpretation and has introduced me to the writings of scholars whose work relates to this theme. Robert Wood Lynn has read most of the manuscript and has also participated with me in a class where some of the ideas were developed. Henry Clark reviewed Chapter II and offered several helpful suggestions. Robert T. Handy took time during the busiest academic season to read the entire manuscript. His careful analysis has improved many sections and clarified or corrected scores of sentences.

William B. Kennedy, now Secretary for Education of the Board of Christian Education of the Presbyterian Church, U.S., was at the time the lectures were delivered Associate Professor of Christian Education at Union Theological Seminary, Richmond, Virginia. In conversations during the lecture series and in reading the material before publication he has helped me relate these ideas to the life of the congregation.

The work these people have devoted to this book must be viewed as an act of friendship rather than an endorsement of the views expressed.

I am also grateful for the many conversations, seminars, and staff meetings in which two other colleagues, Mary Anderson Tully and Marguerite Hyer, have participated; for they have alerted me to many dimensions of religious education that I would have overlooked and have provided an environment in which the most searching questions of communication can be asked. I also remember the kind but insistent voice of Frank Wilber Harriott, who before his retirement reminded me of the need to keep religious education open to the leading of the Spirit of God.

The writing task was made much easier by the efficiency of Mrs. John Redden, who transcribed, typed, and checked the Biblical references for the first draft of this manuscript. I am also grateful to Mrs. David Suh for making the typing of the final copy the first order of business so that it might be completed before she left our office.

C. Ellis Nelson

Union Theological Seminary
in New York

I

Conceptions of Communication

The Christian faith is communicable. Historically, the most descriptive fact about Christianity is its internal compulsion to expand. One has only to scan the book of Acts to feel the driving power of the Apostle Paul and the whole society of believers to evangelize the world. This restlessness of Christianity to expand and to explore is due to its inner nature. Christians believe that God was in Jesus Christ, reconciling the world to himself. When a person experiences the love of God in his inner being, he is free of the stultifying demands of his ego-centered self and is liberated to serve God. He yearns to help others have this same experience. Indeed, the very experience of the love of God creates a divine compulsion in a person to share both himself and his possessions with those who have not yet been liberated from the burden of sin or charged with the sense of divine purpose in their lives.

Probably the oldest manuscript in the New Testament is the Apostle Paul's letter to the church at Thessalonica. In this letter, written about A.D. 48, we find that the church is already a living organization, its members struggling against idols and attempting to be "servants of the living and true God" (1 Thessalonians 1:9, N.E.B.). Paul's concern for this little band of believers is summed up in these words: ". . . may the Lord make your love mount and overflow towards one another and towards all, as our love does towards you" (1 Thessalonians 3:12, N.E.B.). This is the first written record we have of the Christian church. It is steeped in expressions of gratitude for what God had done in Jesus Christ and statements of Christians' obligations to each other and to the world.

To say that faith is communicable is to recognize a fact on which there would be almost universal agreement. But when the question is raised as to *how* it is communicated, the answers are many. If we turn to religious leaders, the answers vary all the way from those on the one hand who say that man can do nothing, absolutely nothing, to communicate faith in God, to those on the other hand who claim to have the keys to the Kingdom and who will guarantee entrance therein to anyone subscribing to a certain creed or living according to a prescribed pattern.

HELP FROM THE SOCIAL SCIENTIST

If we turn to the social scientist and ask how the Christian faith is communicated, the answer is not much better than that supplied by religious leaders. Why? Because social scientists are not in a position to measure faith or trace its path from person to person or group to group, although as observers of the human scene they can evaluate the importance of religious faith as a part of culture. The social scientists who rely on empirical data are not able to locate and domesticate religious faith by the methods they have at their disposal. They can measure religious knowledge and trace its source, but they have not been able to tell us the relationship of religious knowledge to human behavior. Practically all studies that have attempted to relate specific human conduct to religious knowledge have shown that there is no connection that can be demonstrated scientifically. Social scientists can observe human behavior and describe conduct with clarity and honesty, but they have not been able to agree on the motivation for conduct. For example, one can observe stealing in children, count its frequency, and work out the correlation between stealing and the intelligence, social, and economic level, and still not be able to tell why a certain child steals or whether another child will steal. Nor can a clear indication be given of what we can do to create honesty. These studies help us understand human conduct and often make valuable suggestions to us in the church about our work, but they are still at the trial-and-error stage in human affairs in relating motivation to conduct.[1]

The limited value of the empirical social scientists for answering the "how" question must not blind us to the importance of their studies for judging the claims of the church. Studies that show how the church has abandoned people in the inner city, that point out the lack of the church's interest in racial relations, that reveal the shallowness of our morality, that expose the gap between our beliefs and our practices, or the class bias in our preaching and public pronouncements are all proper judgments on the church; and, in that sense, these social scientists are being used by God to modify and correct the church's work. But studies that perform this judgmental role do not give us much help in finding out how faith is communicated, although we can learn how our faith is corrupted and made less effective.

There are other social scientists who do not depend on empirical data alone. Instead, they bring to the problem of human behavior an inquisitive, intuitive mind which formulates questions—questions which can partly be answered by accurate data but which in the end need the imagination and educated guess of a mind grappling with a wide range of observations. This approach is found among many cultural anthropologists, and among sociologists concerned with the way culture is internalized by persons, as well as among psychologists and psychotherapists working with individuals to help them change their behavior. From these social scientists we can find some clues to the way a culture communicates its values to children. They do not attempt to formulate a theory about the communication of Christian faith; but their work gives us important clues to how culture is communicated from one generation to another and how a person internalizes the attitudes, thought patterns, and perceptive system of a culture. Their method, although disciplined and based on careful study, depends on insight and imagination for the formulation of an explanation of how culture is communicated. This method is not greatly different from that used by the great intuitive thinkers of the past. These contemporary social scientists, however, have information about a variety of cultures unknown until the twentieth century, and they are now able to bring to the problems of communication of culture a set of questions and hypotheses that were not considered previously.

The clue that we obtain from these social scientists is the power of the human group, tribe, or subculture to form the basic personality structure of children and the way the social-interactional process among adults formulates questions about, and supplies answers to, the meaning of the past (history), the present (morals, customs, beliefs), and the future (end of history and life after death). The description these social scientists give of how culture at its deepest level is communicated is the closest thing we have to an analysis of how faith is communicated. We have also learned that culture at its deepest levels functions as a religious faith. A study of the process of how adults train children in a culture reveals that deeply held emotional attitudes are engendered as well as the lore of the tribe or subculture. So, these social scientists help us answer our question by showing us that the unit of reality with which we must work in order to understand a process of faith-communication is the group to which a person belongs.

WHY WORRY ABOUT THE QUESTION?

If religious leaders cannot agree on how the Christian faith is communicated and if we get little more than a clue from the social scientists, then why should we concern ourselves about the question? Why should we not accept the limitation of our knowledge and go on with our preaching, teaching, healing, worship, social action, and let whatever communication processes are natural to those activities take place without trying to formulate a theory?

Some leaders in the church go further and say that the communication of faith is so intensely bound up with a mystical experience of God's presence and so highly personal that any systematic study of the process or any attempt to foster the process is the Garden of Eden temptation scene all over again—man trying to get the fruit of the tree of knowledge that doesn't belong to him.

The main idea that underlies these objections is theologically correct. We cannot do any certain thing or combination of things which will communicate faith in God. Our common-sense observation has taught us that stating clearly what Chrisianity is, translating accurately the Bible on which it is based, or even living among Christians will not guarantee that a person receiving this information or these experiences will develop faith in God. Theologically, we must affirm, "For by grace you have been saved through faith; and this is not your own doing, it is the gift of God—not because of works, lest any man should boast" (Ephesians 2:8-9). In this sense faith cannot be communicated, it can only be discovered or evoked.

Although we know God is the source of faith, we also know that he relies on human beings to communicate faith. This leads us to the first reason for attempting to answer the question, "How is faith communicated?" We have an obligation to preach and teach (Matthew 28:18-20) and a commitment to know the truth (John 8:31-32) which require that we form a working theory of *how* we are to communicate the gospel. We do not overlook the facts that the Christian faith has been communicated for centuries without a critical appraisal of the methods used and that it can be communicated today apart from our best-designed programs. In the places where faith is communicated with the most vitality—the Protestant sect groups—the question of "how" is seldom asked. Yet our minds are so constructed that, once it is asked, the question cannot go unanswered. The motive for answering this question is the same motive which underlies our faith: a desire for truth.

Second, we need a conception of communication in order to set goals that will give purpose to our work and by which we can judge our effectiveness. This does not mean that we can clearly define our goals or neatly measure our progress toward them. It does mean that we must have a direction in which we go and a perspective from which we can make decisions about the practical problems we face on our journey.

Within the instructional program of the church a conception of communication is important because it gives a general approach to the curriculum and to the way we use curriculum. Any conscious effort to communicate the Christian faith will have to face problems of Biblical interpretation, use of historical data, the relation of theology to contemporary beliefs, the relation of moral law to actual human conduct, the claims of individuals to a revelatory experience over against the normative belief pattern of the church. These classical problems are basically theological; but because each relates to the present, each participates in the communication process. Any person who has attempted to teach any aspect of the Christian faith at any age level has had to face in any class period one or more of these problems. That is why the practical work of the church in which education is a part can never be the simple application or transmission of theology. The person who communicates is automatically an interpreter and he must have a provisional solution to each of these problems. Thus, the practitioners in the church (pastors, teachers, parents, officers) cannot separate their theology from their efforts to communicate, for each must form and inform the other. Therefore, we must have a way to approach these classic but ever-present problems which is both theologically satisfactory and operationally effective.

We should be equally clear that there is not a utilitarian connection between our conception of communication and specific problems we often face in the instructional work of the church. We cannot move with precision from theology to a particular life problem nor from theory to practice. We cannot, for example, say that a Barthian theology leads by inference to the lecture method, or that a Tillichian theology leads to a discussion method. A practical problem such as the optimum size of a class of Senior High young people cannot be determined by the theology of the Westminster Shorter Catechism. Both Unitarians and Trinitarians use audiovisual methods. We cannot claim that theology will answer all of the specific questions which arise in a local church as we attempt to teach the Christian faith. We can affirm, however, that a theory will give us an approach to all of these specific problems, will help us think critically about our work, and indirectly will suggest ways of doing our work.

If we raise the question of mechanical aids in teaching, then our conception of communication helps us make judgments concerning their use and possible misuse. Teaching machines are not just tools; they embody a theory of learning which must be carefully examined in the light of our conception of faith. Teaching machines train a person to select the right response and reward him instantly for doing so. Thus, the person learns the right answer *and* that he should be rewarded for learning. This procedure has a place in the total scheme of things; but if we believe that faith is an openness to the future and is closely allied with a reprocessing of the past, then learning must help a person to pursue truth critically. Teaching machines, viewed from this perspective, can help us with our efforts to communicate knowledge of faith, but they cannot help us very much in understanding faith personally.

Leadership is another area in which the church must constantly make judgments. Most churches have formalized leadership roles and procedures for selecting professional leaders (ministers, educators, musicians) to interpret and communicate the Christian faith. Although denominations rely heavily on formal educational attainment, such as graduation from a theological seminary, most denominations have other examinations that probe prospective leaders' intentions, religious experiences, and motives for ordination or leadership in the church. These examinations cannot proceed without an underlying conception of what it is that the church desires to communicate and the means to be employed. There are profound problems here which also relate to the lay leaders and lay teachers in a congregation. Are we going to use formal educational attainment or attendance in "leadership" schools as the basis of selection? Shall we select leaders who "get along nicely" with the children? The problem here is not primarily a measurement of the degree to which a person is a good leader but the way he interprets his role as a communicator.

Third, we need a conception of communication in order to understand the particular function of each mode of communication and its interrelation with other modes. Historically, preaching and teaching have been the overt efforts to communicate faith, with worship, healing, and social action as the covert means.

Preaching has declined in importance, but it is still considered to be the first function of the church. Many ministers think of preaching as a presentation of the "word of God," while others consider the sermon as a lecture or as the starting place for discussion groups to be held later.

Teaching is now carried on in a wide variety of agencies ranging all the way from academic institutions with strict controls for the selection of teachers and pupils to the informal, casual gathering of youth groups. Between these extremes we find the teaching of religion in parochial, church, and public schools, in families, and in adult study groups. How shall we find our way through this bewildering array of agencies?

Worship may be our most powerful mode of communication, but how does it fit into a total scheme of things? Does it stand alone as an act of remembrance and gratitude so that all thought and activity of the church flow into it, or is there a relationship between worship, instruction, and social action?

In Protestantism, healing is now almost exclusively related to pastoral care, as we have turned our hospitals over to the state. Because of the unprecedented pressures of modern competitive technical society, the individual has to bear tremendous emotional pressures, and many people have physical and emotional illness as a result. The church has responded to this situation by linking her traditional concern for personal problems with modern psychological knowledge and offers a wide variety of pastoral services. How shall we consider pastoral care as a mode of communication? Should it be domesticated within the church, or should pastoral counselors ally themselves with medical doctors and professional psychologists and move away from the church? If we ask this question from the standpoint of the help individuals may receive for problems, we may say it doesn't make much difference. On the other hand, if we ask how faith can be communicated through, and be involved in, healing, then we may get a different answer.

Social involvement has consisted of service to individuals in need and of action to change the social order. Today in America the social service function of the church has declined while the social action function has increased in importance. Social involvement is primarily an expression of the meaning of faith; but because such involvement shows in a clear and powerful way the difference that faith makes in ordinary life situations in which we all participate, it also communicates faith. Should we then attempt to form and reform persons on the assumption that when they are in their secular work they will help mold social structures so as to bring about justice and equal opportunity? Or should the church work to change the structures of society—laws, customs, economic practices—so that both society and individuals who grow up within it will be different?

The question of how faith is communicated must be answered by everyone who consciously participates in the process. A wide variety of answers has been given, usually in the form of a model. "Models" in this connection are not ideal systems but mental constructions which guide our efforts to communicate in the same way that the model an architect has in mind guides him when he draws his design. A model is a guiding image which puts our beliefs about God, man, church, society, and history in order so we can pass them on to others. A model of communication functions for the communicator as the mental image does for the architect, who must consider the purpose of the building, location, materials, and cost as he draws his design. Similarly, the communicator needs a model which helps him put things in order, suggests a place to start the communication process, tells him what to emphasize, what to expect in the way of results, what should be the role of leadership.

A model is formed in the mind by conscious and unconscious elements. Consciously, we can see the model in our mind and we have an almost automatic, reflex-type connection between the model and what we do. A teacher who has an authoritarian model in mind will, no matter how kindly and considerately, insist on his views against those of the pupil; whereas another teacher with another model in mind may be equally clear in his convictions but may insist that each pupil develop his own views. The unconscious elements come from our personal experiences, especially those in childhood. These elements provide the emotional power which underlies the conscious model. A model of communication expresses deep psychological experiences; that is why educational models are such an explosive topic of conversation. A person who defines or defends a method of teaching is also verbalizing some of his deepest emotional experiences, fears, or longings.

One of the main features of a model of communication is the conception of reality which helps shape the mental image, define the channel of communication, and identify the agency that receives the substance and nature of the message. If we look at the wide variety of models offered in answer to the "how" question, in order to see what the underlying notion of reality is, then we are able to classify models into four broad categories. The clue to finding the idea of reality in each model is to ask, "What is the channel of communication or by what means does a person receive the substance and nature of the message that is to be communicated?" When we answer that question, we find that many diverse models fall into the same category because each answers that question in a similar way.

Perhaps it would be helpful to define four categories. Each category has a common understanding of reality which is shown by the way a person is expected to acquire the Christian faith. Within each category there are many models, but our interest is primarily in the broad definition of each category rather than in the specific characteristics of a model.

It is not the purpose of this book to line up four categories of models, knock down each one in turn, and then offer a fifth that will solve our problems. A fifth category will be offered, but it, too, has problems; it will be offered not because it is a panacea but because it seems closer to the communication of Christian faith, which is assumed to be the reality with which we should be concerned. We shall consider the fifth or "faith-orientation" category later. In this brief review of answers to the *how* question, a few of the strengths and weaknessess of these answers will be pointed out from the faith perspective.

Communication Through the Mind

Some models of communication are built on the assumption that reality is in ideas and that the mind is the agency for receiving and transmitting the meaning of faith. These models emphasize in varying degree the importance of religious knowledge or doctrine. Preaching and teaching tend to be explanations of doctrine. Communication leans heavily on the conscious, logical processes of the mind. Ethical and moral problems are considered soluble by the proper application of religious belief.

We must be careful not to assume that the doctrinal approach is limited to conservative or creedal churches. It is an approach that can be used by Trinitarians and Unitarians, by churches with congregational polity, or by sects that have no professional clergy or sacramental system. All that is needed is the presupposition, implicit or explicit, that certain beliefs *must* be held as an expression of faith in God and that a person's mind is the chief channel of communication.

Models of communication which give priority to the mind have the advantage of bringing clarity to a belief system. The mind is the location of our self-consciousness, the instrument by which we form language and interpret our experiences. The mind is central in any form of communication; therefore, it is sensible and efficient to use this means of communication to pass on our knowledge of God. Parents and teachers who live close to children can see their minds growing, searching, and developing confidence. Instructing a person's mind at this early stage of development is relatively easy and is important for future maturity.

There is a tendency, however, for models built on the reality of the mind to make faith synonymous with knowledge or "right doctrine." We know that God is not a creed, idea, or doctrine. The Incarnation, whatever form of doctrine it may take, indicates that God in his finest revelation was in Jesus and not primarily in the human mind. The mind is an instrument of understanding, rather than the source of Christian truth. Then, too, the mental approach —focusing attention on knowledge and ideas—is not able to handle concrete life situations. One cannot move from general principles to practical problems deductively because there is a stubbornness about the facts and conditions of any human situation which causes us to qualify general ideas. Honesty, it is generally agreed, is a desirable principle, but the facts in many specific human situations make us qualify that general principle. It is this inability of the world of the mind, where control and order are possible, to get to the world of human events, where contingencies of many kinds come into play, which limits the usefulness of models of communication that start with and depend on the mind.

Communication Through Experience

This category of models considers experience to be the central reality, and contemporary experience, either by an individual or a group, to be the main agency of communication. The focus is on the present, so group discussion of human problems often becomes the method of work. Although preaching and teaching in the conventional sense may be used, this approach assumes that these or any other methods which transmit ideas or information from the past are chiefly useful in developing resources to be used by a contemporary group.

Some models in this category emphasize contemporary social experience as the place where God is at work: communication takes place as we participate in activities that change attitudes or create new attitudes toward the social order. Other models insist on the necessity of a personal conversion experience, saying that from this experience one learns how to serve God in the social order.

From the standpoint of faith, models in this category have many assets. Faith is experiential, so the emphasis on experience in human situations is broader than that of the mind. Our human experience includes hope, fear, sin, forgiveness, accidents, evil, death, ambitions, and many other elements. Moreover, the insistence on experience as a central reality around which our communication models can be built makes it possible to use ideas and insights from psychologists and other social scientists who study human behavior. Also, a focus on current experience forces a reconsideration of all our historically rooted forms and practices and requires that we find God's truth afresh for our generation.

On balance, though, we have to admit that when experience is absolutized, it makes the present more important than the past, and we cannot understand ourselves that way. In order to know ourselves, we must know our history so that we may gain a perspective in understanding the forces that shaped our present. A preoccupation with personal religious experience, important as it may be, is likely to produce a religion oriented to "personal needs." This would violate the Biblical demand that man is to obey God by the way he serves the needs of his fellow men. A preoccupation with social experience on the assumption that man's ills are socially induced is likely to overlook the greed, pride, and ambition in individuals which have marked every primitive or civilized people of which we have a record. Experience, in itself, is an incomplete notion on which to develop a conception of communication.

Communication Through Selfhood

The vagueness and difficulty which plague other models of communication—such as the relationship of tradition to revelation, faith to reason, the person to society, law to grace—can be cleared up if we look at the person as a living, dynamic unity which overrides these polarities. The person, with his needs and possibilities, is a practical and profound place to start the development of a theory of communication. We experience life as a person, and it is natural to assume that selfhood is the basic reality. If we want a model that will give us a way to handle most of the perplexing problems of communication, including the utilization of psychological and sociological data along with theology, then selfhood models will be more rewarding than any of the others.

Some models in the selfhood category see God as having a reality like that of a person and the communication between God and man as that of a self to another self. Other models see the God-man relationship as one in which God helps a person achieve a "whole" self out of the frustrations and difficulties of life. Salvation in this case comes when a person is able to live "authentically" without external moralistic requirements.

Selfhood as the central reality for communication has a natural appeal. People feel that they can do something about themselves and influence other selves, especially children, even when they are powerless to affect social or political institutions in any important way.

As desirable as the goal of self-realization is, we must question —from the faith standpoint—the validity of such a goal. We have no Biblical illustrations of a person's being blessed by God because of his psychological wholeness. Rather, the hero of the Bible stories is the person who does the will of God; and the degree of personal help he receives is always a subordinate feature of the story.

We must also question the priority of the self. One of the clearest affirmations developed by the social scientists in the twentieth century is the role of society in shaping the self. The self cannot be isolated from society except in a clinical setting, and even there the psychotherapist works to help the self adjust to its social environment. The self is, in part, the product of society; before we can understand why a self is like it is, we have to understand the society that shaped it. This means that we have to deal not only with society but with the history that conditioned the society. The self, in short, does not stand alone but is a particle in the stream of history. When we see our problem this way, then the power of the self as a reality for communicating the Christian faith wanes in the face of the power of history and of social systems.

Communication Through the Church

The church formed as a result of Christ's resurrection has endured, expanded, and continues to be in its various institutional manifestations the agency which fosters and forms the Christian faith. The church as a social organization is unique. No other social organization has lived so long or is so widespread today as is the Christian church. Beliefs about the nature of the church range all the way from the idea that it is an extension of the Incarnation to the idea that it is a gathering of individuals who give allegiance to Christ. Regardless of belief about its nature, the church is the institution that attempts to communicate the Christian religion.

Models of communication based on the church are attractive. The church as a social organism can maintain itself even if it is not able to work out all of the intellectual polarities (such as the relation between faith and reason) to which we have referred. Moreover, the membership of the church can live with tensions caused by practical situations, such as the quarreling between rival but equally sincere parties of believers who interpret faith differently, or tensions caused by the ethical stand of the church on matters such as divorce or war. The loyalty of the believers to

Christ can bridge intellectual and practical rifts because the church offers a perspective which plays down the purely temporal and subordinates conflict to the greater good of the whole church.

One is tempted to describe the ideal church from New Testament sources and then develop a model of communication which would help produce such a church. But we must remember that the church in the New Testament was not ideal and that the history of the church reveals as much of man's sin as it does of God's grace and guidance. When the church is used as a central reality around which we build a model of communication, there is a tendency to make the church as an institution the goal of the communication process. Education tends to become a process of creating loyalty to the institution, of inculcating a penitential system that requires the constant ministry of the clergy, or of making the layman into a churchman. This focus of concern on the church also tends to separate the church from the world and to create a ghetto mentality, so that the ordinary affairs of life, especially the structures of society, are connected to the church only as matters about which we pray. We tend to forget that the church is also under judgment, is also capable of sin, and is in constant need of guidance from the Spirit of God.

When the church is considered to be the institutional expression of truth, we tend also to rely too heavily on the authority of church leaders or to assume that whatever is done in the church is right. We do not take seriously the possibility of truth from other quarters. The testimony of the Bible is that God is not bound by Israel or by the church and that the truth can come from many sources.

ANOTHER STARTING PLACE

I said earlier it is not my intention to set up four straw men and then knock each down and present a fifth that can withstand criticism. Each of the four categories has virtues as indicated, but each also has tendencies within it (because of its central idea of reality) which give us difficulty in shaping a model of communication.

Our problem is further complicated because models in each of the four categories can work fairly well in actual practice. That is why any discussion of the means of communication of the faith is subject to argument and difference of opinion. Devotees of any one model can cite case after case where their method produced fine, intelligent Christians. These claims are not doubted. It is possible in a single congregation to find teachers following models from all four categories. In one class a teacher may be intent on teaching doctrine; in another room a leader may be busy with activities because he feels that the students learn only through direct social participation; in another place a minister may be helping an individual work through his religious beliefs, while in still in another segment of the same congregation the communicants' class may be taught from the point of view of the church as a holy institution. Moreover, it is highly probable that the persons who implicitly or explicitly use a certain model *are actually communicating faith by a different means.* For example, the teacher who follows a doctrine model may be the kind of person who in his personal relationship with his pupils exhibits a loving concern for them and for other people; and this may be the element in his life with which the pupils identify and which they seek to appropriate, rather than the logic of his doctrine.

Even though each of the four has excellent points in its favor, we cannot select the good points in each and put them together to make a different model. Rather, we have to ask ourselves: What is the reality we want to communicate, and what is the natural agency for communicating that reality?

FAITH AS A CATEGORY OF COMMUNICATION

The answer we want to explore in this study is that faith in the God described in the Bible is the reality around which we should plan our model and that the natural agency of communication is the community of believers. We shall explore and expand this proposition in the following chapters but at this point will simply indicate that the Bible is primarily a book about the faith of a people. Although it contains a variety of types of literature, covers several thousand years of history, and deals with a wide variety of problems, the central topic throughout the Bible is faith. The eleventh chapter of Hebrews is a retelling of the history of Israel as a story of faith—not only in terms of exploits for God, but also that "by faith we understand" (Hebrews 11:3a); and the twelfth chapter continues the story, urging that we see in Jesus "the pioneer and perfecter of our faith" (Hebrews 12:2a). Equally clear is the assumption that faith is communicated by the community of believers. In the Old Testament, faith is not welded to Israel; many Israelites left the nation and the nation itself was split, but there was always a remnant which was faithful to God and that remnant was the incubator of true faith. Likewise, in the New Testament the church is the corporate unity which propagates faith; yet faith is not confined to the church, as the story of Cornelius shows (Acts 10), nor is everyone in the church a person of faith, as the story of Ananias and Sapphira indicates (Acts 5:1-11).

Even a brief review of the history of the church since the New Testament days would require that we note many mistakes the church has made: the alliance of the church with forces of evil such as slavery, the ambitions of church leaders, the many times the churches worked out treaties with secular rulers in order to gain institutional advantages, and so on. But throughout this same history, we will also find men of faith struggling against ecclesiastical authority as Luther did or struggling to gain a vision of God's will for evangelizing foreign lands as William Carey did; and when the balance is struck between these two forces in church history, the men of faith stand out as the ones who have led the church and the world to a clearer understanding of God's purpose. In so doing, they also redefined the *meaning* of the Christian faith.

A moment with our own experience would confirm the proposition that there is a sentiment lying deep within us which is the reality of our religion.[2] Although pushed by adversaries or buffeted by intellectual doubts, we are still a part of the believing community as long as we can say, "I believe; help thou mine unbelief" (Mark 9:24, k.j.v.). We have experienced enough shift in our own belief-system as we grew up and enough change in theological formulations in recent generations to be aware that underlying all of our rational efforts to explain our religion is faith.

We must be careful to note that we are not talking about the doctrine of "justification by faith." In fact, the history of that doctrine after the Reformation is a good illustration of what happens when we attempt to absolutize faith. Although Martin Luther made a brilliant appropriation of Paul's words that "the righteous shall live by faith" (Romans 1:17b) and was able to break away from the shackle of a legalistic, penitential system and find his salvation in Christ by faith alone, a hundred years later Protestantism had formalized the doctrine of faith into a new dogma which was almost as restrictive as the dogma it replaced. Although faith is involved in doctrine, experience, selfhood, and the church, faith is different in that it cannot be absolutized. By its nature faith is open, expectant, guided but not controlled by the past. Faith, in short, is the description of a relationship to God, and it derives its meaning from the object of that relationship—God.

The faith we shall discuss is not faith as a psychological phenomenon. We shall always have in mind faith in "the God of the Bible" as a point of reference for this discussion. The term "God of the Bible" is in itself an ambiguous term; it needs a considerable amount of clarification, which will be attempted as we go along in our discussion. For the moment, let us be content to say that the identification of the God of the Bible means that we have a reliable description of God in relation to past events, that the Bible is a record of how God related himself to his people and his world, and that so defined, God functions in the same way today even though the human situation is in many ways sharply different from that described in the Bible. Although our conception of God is rooted in the past, God is free to be what he wants to be today; hence the Christian's central concern is to be a learner of God's will for current events. Faith is, therefore, not only the relationship of trust between the believer and God: it is also—on the doctrinal side—constantly undergoing critical review and constantly being reconceptualized. Faith, we propose, can be the reality about which we can formulate a conception of communication.

NEW PROBLEMS

On the surface it may seem that to start with faith and to make the formation of faith central in a conception of communication will neatly answer our question of "how to communicate" by avoiding all of the sharply defined problems in the communication process. Indeed, some people say that it doesn't make much difference what we do "if we have faith": our efforts, no matter how clumsy or ill informed, if pleasing to God, will be blessed. Theologically, we may defend that statement in order to defend the freedom of God to do what he wants to do and to make all kinds of peculiar circumstances serve his purposes; but as a practical matter this statement denies the use of our God-given powers of reason. Our piety is to be shown in our use of intelligence—not in avoiding the problems inherent in communication; so we shall not use faith as a way to avoid our problems.

By making faith the central thrust of our conception we compound our problems. We are dealing with an entity which is notoriously vague, and consequently we will have much more difficulty finding a starting place that has the same visibility and concreteness as is found in the other four categories. Moreover, in our tentative description of faith in the God of the Bible we have already indicated that this view requires us to be open, since God is free. Thus, we do not have the assurance and reassurance associated with one of the other starting places; for they present us with a reality that is present, whereas faith is involved in the immediacy of events moving into an uncertain future. Such a stand is possible only to a person of some maturity, and this presents us with an agonizing problem of readiness. When is a person ready for faith? Out of what kind of experience can such a faith-experience be developed? Can children develop faith in these terms or is faith something that has to be held "in trust" by parents? In each of the other four categories we can develop ways of communicating with children separately from adults, often in schools, because the medium of communication is applicable, with proper adaptations, to children. The faith approach requires experience and judgment beyond the capacity of children. There is no way we can scale these elements down so that they can be put into the curriculum for children. We shall have to work on all of these special problems, particularly in the last chapter, where we will sketch out some practical implications of this approach to communication of the Christian faith.

Not only does this approach present us with the vagueness and uncertainty that surround faith, but also the human source of faith, the community of believers, is difficult to define sharply or to categorize neatly. Our first impulse would be to say the church is the community of believers, but it has already been indicated that we must resist that temptation. God is not limited to the church as an institution, nor is he dependent upon official church leadership. A community of believers could be a small group of concerned individuals within a congregation. It could be a denomination that is obedient to the lordship of Christ. It could be a residential community that is determined to hold all things in common, such as the Society of Brothers, or a Protestant order such as the one located in Taizé, France. It could have many manifestations. What a community of believers *must* have is face-to-face personal relations of enough permanence for the group to worship, work, and study together under a common commitment to the God of the Bible even though their interpretation of that God varies from person to person. What they have in common is faith, with all that implies in commitment, concern for each other, and responsibility for the community in which they live. This could be a congregation of a denomination, but it is not restricted to that type of gathering. It is, however, in every case a group in which individuals are actively interacting with each other in many of the dimensions and interests of life.

In short, then, this book proposes to sketch an answer to the question of *how* the Christian faith is communicated by assuming that faith in the God of the Bible is the basic reality we want to share and that this is done through a community of believers. This category, from which several models could be developed, is suggested not because it promises to provide practical procedures for communication but because it seems better to represent the full implication of the communication process of which the Bible is a report and because it conforms to much of our modern knowledge and experience of how faith is transmitted from one generation to another.

II

The Formative Power of Culture

In the first chapter we suggested that the social scientists, who study culture and the process whereby a society transmits its beliefs to succeeding generations, offer us a clue in developing models for the communication of faith. To open up this discussion, we must analyze the process by which human life is formed by, and lived in, social units. Most of this chapter will describe how this process operates. Although some illustrations from our religious life will be used, the purpose at this point is not to be prescriptive; that will come later.

DEFINITION OF TERMS

In order to analyze the process of communication inherent in society we must first have a working definition of major terms. This is by no means easy. The social sciences are all so new and so bound up with the personal viewpoint of the individual scholar that we can seldom find an exact definition which has come into common usage. However, we can find considerable common agreement on broad definitions of basic elements in a society, and this will be satisfactory for our purposes.

There are three major elements in any society that are interrelated and mutually dependent yet can be separated for analytical purposes. These elements are culture, society, and individual. No one has worked out a clear, generally accepted statement of how these three elements are interrelated. Indeed, few social scientists have tried to unravel these elements even in a relatively homogeneous primitive society. But they have been able to separate these elements in such a way that we can see clearly how each element functions in a society; and, allowing for some inaccuracy because of the complexity of the human community, we can see how culture trains—"educate" is too soft a word here—individuals and the extent to which and the manner in which individuals can influence the nature and goals of society.[1]

Culture. Let us start with culture because it is the most pervasive element. A culture may continue historically even though a society disintegrates. According to Ralph Linton, a culture is the way of life of a society; it is a guide to how the individual should act in various circumstances.[2] Linton's formal definition states that "A culture is the configuration of learned behavior and results of behavior whose component elements are shared and transmitted by the members of a particular society."[3] By this definition, he makes the communication process the distinctive characteristic of culture. Anything that is strictly private and not generally passed on to others is not culture, although to the individual it may be an important and necessary part of his life. Also, note that what is passed on is called "the configuration of learned behavior," by which Linton means what other social scientists call "patterned behavior." Normally, a culture transmits a pattern of action to individuals for a variety of life situations. Many of these patterns are for the individual in his everyday activity; some are reserved for birth, puberty, courtship, marriage, and death. By "results of behavior" Linton means the social values and attitudes and general knowledge of the world that a person acquires as he is nurtured in a society, plus all of the objects that are made and used by a society. In short, one can define a culture when he is able to describe the behavior patterns of a particular people, understand the attitudes and values associated with these actions, and understand the objects made and used by the people of a given culture.

Charles Winick defines culture as "All that which is non-biological and socially transmitted in a society including artistic, social, ideological, and religious patterns of behavior and the techniques for mastering the environment."[4] To state it negatively, culture is what a person would not learn if he were alone. Jurgen Ruesch expresses the same central idea in these words: "Culture [is] the accumulated body of the knowledge of the past, continued in memories and assumptions of people who express their knowledge in definite ways."[5]

These definitions are extremely broad; yet they separate culture from society or the individual. If we wanted to define culture more sharply, we would say that the value system is the most important element in a culture. It is only when we know the values of a culture that we are able to understand the reasons why people act, think, and work the way they do; and we shall examine the way values determine human conduct later in this chapter.

Society. A society is the organized part of life. It is different from culture and from the individual in that it is a system in which roles must be played, work assigned, responsibilities fixed, and laws or regulations made, interpreted, and enforced. Individuals do all of these things and they can exercise their individuality in all of these roles; but society as such is not just a collection of individuals—it is a reality that keeps on going even when the individual dies or refuses to play his role therein. The phrase "culture is the way of life of a society" can be turned around to state that "a society is the way people are organized to express the values of their culture." In this sense, a society is the government of a group of people. There can be various governmental units which share a common culture. An example of a society would be a nation or a governmental subunit such as a city.

A family is not a society, although it has some of the qualities of a society, such as different work assignments to the individuals in the family and rewards and punishments given to individuals according to the way they behave. A family is not a society because as a unit it does not have continuity: new families are formed, but particular families die out. Also, the relationship within families is highly personal, whereas in a society relationships are impersonal. If a political leader is killed he is replaced, for that role in a society must be played; but if an individual in a family is killed, he as a person cannot be replaced. This distinction is an important one. On the one hand, the family is one of the most important units for communicating faith and the meaning of faith. On the other hand, we cannot work out a system of Christian nurture based on the family alone because the family is more an agent of culture and society than it is an independent unit. We cannot assume that society can be "family-like, only bigger." The difference between the family and society is a difference in kind rather than in degree or size. We must watch this point carefully. There is always a tendency to assume that the problems of society would be solved if we could just expand the virtues of the family to the society.

Primary Society. All societies, primitive and modern, are made up of many small organized or semiorganized groups of people. These primary societies are most effective in transmitting the cultural patterns of thought and action, in forming the selfhood of individuals, and in providing a place where the individual can establish and maintain a style of life different from that of the surrounding culture. The United States has thousands of primary societies such as work or friendship groups, churches, lodges, community groups, clubs, and others. Very often the primary societies are formed by, and are expressions of, social class values. Here we must note that the family is not a primary society because primary societies are formed voluntarily and, in the case of fraternal orders, churches, and other groups, can become societies which exercise discipline and control over the members. Also, primary societies are usually made up of adults; if children are part of the group, they are considered to be in training for adult roles in that particular group.

Individual. The individual in all societies, primitive and modern, has an area of thought and action which is peculiar to himself. Within that area an individual is able to express a wide variety of personal choices and to develop new or creative patterns of action. The idea that a primitive society is homogeneous has been shown to be false by anthropologists who have lived for a period of time with primitive people. Moreover, the range of personality types, insofar as a rough classification scheme can be formulated, is found to be as wide in primitive as in modern Western societies.

Although this general statement outlines a certain amount of freedom for the individual and allows for a person's expressing himself in unique ways, we must not give the impression that a person will be able easily or quickly to become something other than what he is. A primitive tribe which believes in witchcraft will produce individuals who believe in witchcraft, although individuals may make innovations in the practice of witchcraft.

The important matter for our purpose is the distinction we must make between the individual, culture, and society. Although individuals make up society, society is formed to meet the general needs of a group; and these needs are different from those of the individual. For example, justice is a need of a group of people: a murderer is punished, although as an individual the murderer would like to go unpunished. Individuals have wants and needs based on their physical and psychological makeup, but culture has general values related to what a group of human beings wants. Individuals know the difference between the two. In fact, much of a person's inner struggle is caused by the clash between what he wants as an individual and what his society will let him have. Society almost always wins the struggle. For example, an individual normally wants to preserve his life; yet if society requires that he go to war, the individual usually goes and thus places his life in jeopardy.

It may be helpful at this point to give a general illustration of these distinctions. A Presbyterian middle-class teen-ager raised in a conservative church in a southern city will probably be more like a Scots middle-class teen-ager raised in a conservative church in Scotland than the American Presbyterian teen-ager will be like a liberal Jewish teen-ager raised in the same southern town. In this case, the southern town presents us with the same society for the Jewish and the Presbyterian teen-ager. However, the primary society (conservative Presbyterian church) interprets a religious tradition (Calvinism) in such a way that another teen-ager raised in a similar religious environment, though it be four thousand miles away, will be more like the American Presbyterian than the latter will be like his liberal Jewish fellow citizen.

CULTURAL REALITY

The definitions given above for each of the elements in our ongoing human experience are offered for analytical purposes only. In actual life it is difficult, if not impossible, to separate these elements. Social scientists do not yet have a clear idea of how each element interpenetrates the other or how changes in society or culture are made under the influence of new circumstances or unusual leaders. What is known is that culture is internalized in persons and institutionalized in society. Culture is the meaning of life that is transmitted to others, especially to children. It is a belief system that is taught with emotional conviction and urgency. Culture is also what others—especially children—ought to believe, so it presents us with patterns of behavior and thought that we are expected to follow. The culture of America is both formed by and interpreted by the thousands of primary societies in which people participate as individuals and as family units. For our purposes we shall deal with culture and with primary societies, for it is these elements that form the individual. It is in the primary societies that the individual comes into selfhood and through which he exercises his most direct influence on culture and society. The organized structure of society in governmental units is important, but for our purpose we shall assume that society will reflect in laws and governmental agencies the values and social goals that are developed by the culture.

Why is culture, as communicated through primary societies, families, and individuals, a reality with which we must deal?

Culture is a reality that endures.   Although we experience life as individuals, we live our lives in groups and we develop our selfhood only as we interact with others. Moreover, as adults we can satisfy our physical and psychological needs only as we associate ourselves with others. We realize early that we have come into a stream of human culture, that we will someday drop out of that stream, that the stream flows on. In our sober moments of thought, we know that our primary societies and families perpetuate "our kind of" culture. This is why we give ourselves to these groups— in order to change or maintain the way of life we hold dear. Since the individual cannot survive forever, the only way he can influence the future is through primary societies, through the family, and through his individual participation in society.

Culture forms selfhood.   The moment a person is born he is surrounded with culture. Culture has already decided who will take care of him, how he will be dressed, fed, and handled. Long before he has any self-consciousness, his selfhood is shaped by culture. It is true that the individual responds and slowly builds his own selfhood; but this can be done only in relation to other people who surround him—his family and others from the various primary societies with which his family associates. Although it is easy to state this point, it is relatively difficult to understand its full implication unless one has lived for a time in a culture other than his own. Observing there how naturally a child learns to do things that seem "wrong," one will have had the experience of realizing how his own unargued assumptions about life are not the assumptions of people in a different culture.

Culture teaches the individual. Culture does more than supply the "given" to which a person must react: culture does a lot of direct teaching of the individual in the family and in primary societies. This direct teaching is not only about the situations that the person faces but also about hypothetical situations the culture thinks will arise. This is different from random learning that may take place. The direct teaching is necessary in order for the society to maintain itself, and the socializing agents see that the child develops these patterns of behavior. In a primary society the child is told how to handle himself in situations which may occur. Linton states the matter in these words: "The way in which a person responds to a particular situation often provides a better clue to what his teaching has been than to what his personality is."[6] What the adults who surround the child believe is right is a more articulate and dynamic part of his life than is the part that is consciously fashioned.

On the surface, this seems to be a gross exaggeration. We usually compare ourselves with our parents and other early socializers on the basis of our superior knowledge, income, or status. But if we look at areas of our lives which develop out of interpersonal relations—such as our deference to people in authority, our ability to forgive, our ability to share our affection, or our ability to handle new and unexpected human situations with self-confidence and intelligence—then we will probably realize the truth of Linton's statement. The word "taught" means in this connection the direct instruction by a combination of words, examples, promise of rewards, or threat of punishments.

Culture defines the goals and methods of society. Since we have already said we do not know exactly how culture and society are interrelated, we cannot at this point do more than make the general observation that, in the main, culture defines the goals and methods that a society as an organized system expresses. On the other hand, society as an organized structure can sometimes control cultural developments. Only in specific situations can we judge the relation between these two elements. For example, cultural values and society are in sharp conflict in the United States around the civil rights issue. For a long time a general cultural value has been shaping up which would require that Negroes have equal rights with other races. This value has now become a part of American society through recent Supreme Court rulings and civil rights legislation. Society, as expressed in state governments in some areas, has used its powers to resist both the new cultural value that has developed and the laws of the larger society. However, the laws of the larger society have put pressure on state governments, individuals, and churches so that change toward racial integration in education, employment, and housing is also changing the cultural values to support this new condition. In general, culture is the element that determines the nature and purposes of society; changes in culture are necessary before lasting changes in society are possible. Normally, culture is the reality with which we must deal if we want to be influential in the shaping of individuals or of society.

WHAT CULTURE COMMUNICATES

If culture is the reality that has gone into the bones of our being before we were conscious that it was there, what is communicated? To say that everything we are was given to us by culture is too general a statement. It will not help us to say that culture is an answer to the question, "What is the meaning of life?" Religion also claims to answer this question. In the more homogeneous primitive cultures or in a theocracy, such as that represented by the Hebrews in the Old Testament, culture and religion serve together to express the meaning of life. In our pluralistic society, culture and religion can be separated, and this presents us with a complex situation. Culture continues to function as a religion in that it provides an answer to the question of the meaning of life, yet religion claims to answer the same question. There is obviously an overlapping of answers.

In America one can find relatively homogeneous Protestant communities where the culture of the local community and the Protestant religion are practically the same. One also can find in large metropolitan areas a general cultural pattern that is shared only in part by small Protestant sects. It is an assumption of this book that America is increasingly becoming a secular, pluralistic, urban society and that the Protestant ethos which dominated when the Constitution was written is no longer the ethos of the country generally.[7] It is further assumed that the Christian faith is based on a revelation from God which transcends culture and comes into human life for the purpose of directing human culture. It is essential, therefore, that we explore what culture communicates in order to separate *to some extent* the Christian tradition from culture.

World View

Men have always thought about the world in which they lived, creating myths concerning its origin, purpose, and future. A child coming into self-consciousness must have an explanation of the world around him; the primary society provides the explanation that he needs in order to feel at home in the animate and inanimate world he experiences. It is important to say "the world he experiences" because the child does not really experience the world as it is but as his socializers say it is. He is able to make sense out of the world because a meaningful story of the world is supplied, and he is taught to select from his sense experience the kind of data that "proves" the "truth" of the myths that he has heard.

Often a culture will link its world view with God, but this it not always the case. In some cultures God is unrelated to the world, and in some cultures religion is unrelated to a god, as in Buddhism. Regardless of how God is thought to be connected or disconnected with the world, there are myths about the world and the relation of man to the world. A good part of a person's selfhood is intensely tied up with his world view. The myths he believes about the world are extensions of himself; to shake that mythical world view is to shake the person to the core of his being.

Dorothy Lee describes the Wintu Indians of northern California as living in an area so densely wooded that it is difficult to find clear land for building shelter; yet the Wintu will not cut down timber—they use only dead wood. They will not use a plow because a plow would hurt the earth; rather, they make little holes for their planting. When they kill a deer, they eat it all, not because they are frugal but because they respect the animals. When they use rocks, they choose small rocks so as not to hurt the earth. Lee continues: "Here we find people who do not so much *seek* communion with environing nature as *find themselves* in communion with it. . . . Here, man is *in* nature already, and we cannot speak properly of man *and* nature."[8]

Robert Redfield has reminded us that a people's world view is the way the world looks to them and the way they are to live in relation to this world. "It is that organization of ideas which answers to a man the questions: Where am I? Among what do I move? What are my relations to those things?"[9]

Leslie A. White has described the world of the Pueblo Indians in these words:

> The world of the Pueblo Indians was not created in the beginning; it was always there—or here. But it was somewhat different in the beginning than it is now. The Earth was square and flat; it had four corners and a middle. Below the surface of the earth there were four horizontal layers; each one was a world. The lowest world was a white one. Above that lay the red world and then the blue one. Above the blue world, and just beneath this world that we are living in today, was the yellow world.
>
> In the beginning the people were living deep down inside the earth, in the white world, with their mother, Iyatiku. Finally it was time for them to come out, to ascend to this world. Iyatiku caused a great evergreen tree, a spruce or a fir, to grow so that the people could climb up its trunk and boughs to the next world. But when the tree reached the next world above it found its way blocked by a hard layer of earth and rock. So Iyatiku had Woodpecker make a hole through the layer into the next world. The people

climbed up into the red world and lived there for four years. Then it was time to climb up into the blue world. Again Iyatiku had a tree reach up to the world above, and again she had someone make a hole through the hard layer so the tree and the people could pass through.

At last the people were ready to ascend into this world. Iyatiku had Badger make a hole through the hard crust. He made so much dust in his work that there was danger that the people might be blinded, so Whirlwind Old Man went up and held the dust in his arms until Badger got through. Then Cicada was asked to line the opening so it would be smooth and safe to pass through. Iyatiku asked Badger to look out into this world and tell her what it looked like. Badger looked out. "It is very beautiful up there," he told Iyatiku, "there are rain clouds everywhere." So Iyatiku decided it was all right for the people to complete their ascent and to emerge into this world. Iyatiku had created societies of medicine men in the lower worlds and had given them their altars and ceremonies. These societies—the Flint, Fire, Giant, and Kapina medicine men—came out with the people. There were some evil spirits, too, who also came out. They were *kanadyaiya,* 'witches,' but no one knew this at that time.[10]

White continues his discussion of the Pueblo Indians, showing how they account for the hardness of the soil, the importance of corn as a food, the origin of rain, the abundance of small game, and all the other things the Indians experienced in the world of the American southwest.

The Christian religion has formed its world view largely from the stories in Genesis to account for the creation of the world, man's situation of disobedience, and God's command that man use the animate and inanimate world about him. This general world view is given more specific content in the salvation story of the New Testament, which was incorporated into the Apostles' Creed, one of the earliest creeds and today the most widely used. The Apostles' Creed has often been criticized because it omits practically all references to the ethical demands of the Christian faith and to the teachings of Jesus. The Creed does not emphasize Christian life because it is primarily a world view, a belief system that orders the relation of God to man in salvation, and a description of the unseen world.

THE APOSTLES' CREED

I believe in God the Father Almighty, Maker of heaven and
earth;

And in Jesus Christ His only Son our Lord; who was conceived
by the Holy Ghost, born of the Virgin Mary, suffered under
Pontius Pilate, was crucified, dead, and buried; He descended into
hell; the third day He rose again from the dead; He ascended into
heaven, and sitteth on the right hand of God the Father Almighty;
from thence He shall come to judge the quick and the dead.

I believe in the Holy Ghost; the holy Catholic Church; the
communion of saints; the forgiveness of sins; the resurrection of
the body; and the life everlasting. Amen.

The culture's world view is mediated directly to the child by his
socializers, usually his parents, and it becomes an integral part of
his self-understanding. Unless that world view is challenged, the
person will see the world only as he was instructed. If his view is
challenged or if he grows up in a culture where a variety of world
views are clamoring for attention, he will have to make some kind
of adjustment. A person does not feel comfortable without an
explanation of his environment. In any case, a person's world view
and his values—both of which come from his culture—will be
interrelated and will function together in directing his actions. The
following illustration will help us see how practical this analysis is
in understanding human actions.

Erik H. Erikson and Mekeel made a study of the Sioux Indians
which was, in part, an examination of the expectations of our
society—the American view that the past is something we can
overcome, that by our efforts we can achieve, that a higher standard of living lies ahead if we plan and work for it. This viewpoint
is seen in the federally appointed civil service educator who assumed that the Sioux Indians would want to have a home, fire-
place, and bank account. The Indian, however, had his own view
based on his historical memory of the buffalo hunter. He had a self-
image infused with the tribal glory of the past when the Sioux had
been free, space was unlimited, and the supply of buffalo was inex-
haustible. Although now a member of a conquered tribe, the Indian's vision of the past was so powerful that he unconsciously

dreamed that the past would be restored someday and that he would become what he knew deep within himself he really was. The clash of these two world views within his soul resulted in a passive resistance to the efforts of the white conqueror to educate him into an American world view.[11]

After making a study of the political involvement of Buddhists in Vietnam, Dennis W. Morgan comments on the self-burning of monks protesting government policies. These suicides left Americans with feelings of revulsion and horror; in our view, conditions can never become so bad that they may not change, and even if conditions do not change, Americans generally believe that a person should not willingly take the life God has given him. We believe that only God is to judge the time of death and that we are to prolong life by every conceivable means. We think of suicide as self-destruction due to cowardice or despair. However, in the Buddhist view the self-burning is not suicide.

> Those monks who burned themselves to death did it to call attention to the suffering endured by the Vietnamese and to seek to move their oppressors to relent. The monks believe that to say something while experiencing the extreme pain of burning is, in the words of Thich Nhat Hanh, "to say it with the utmost of courage, frankness, determination, and sincerity. . . . The Vietnamese monk, by burning himself, says with all his strength and determination that he can endure the greatest of sufferings to protect his people." The fact that the monk burns himself to death is incidental in the light of his belief in the continuous cycle of rebirths, and he expects his self-sacrifice to benefit his people.[12]

The Buddhist world view, combined with Buddhist social values, gave the Buddhist monks who immolated themselves a different pattern of action from that of the American Christian.

However, the Americanized Christian view is not the same view we find in the writings of the Apostle Paul. Or, perhaps we should say our interpretation of the Biblical view is different from that of the Apostle Paul. You will remember that Paul came to the conclusion that Jesus would soon return to bring in a new messianic age. This belief was so central to Paul's thought that it permeated his whole theological system; we cannot begin to interpret his writing until we have comprehended what it was like to believe that the world would soon end. In writing to the church in Corinth, Paul had to answer many specific questions about how to act in a variety of situations, for example, marriage. Because of the "impending distress" Paul recommended that his readers not marry. This is logical advice if one believes that "the appointed time has grown very short . . . For the form of this world is passing away" (1 Corinthians 7:25-31).

> Erikson uses the term "ideological system" to mean a coherent body of shared images, ideas, and ideals which (whether based on a formulated dogma, an implicit *Weltanschauung*, a highly structured world image, a political creed, or a "way of life") provides for the participants a coherent, if systematically simplified, over-all orientation in space and time, in means and ends.[13]

> . . . All ideologies ask for, as the prize for the promised possession of a future, uncompromising commitment to some absolute hierarchy of values and some rigid principle of conduct: be that principle total obedience to tradition, if the future is the eternalization of ancestry; total resignation, if the future is to be of another world; total martial discipline, if the future is to be reserved for some brand of armed superman; total inner reform, if the future is perceived as an advanced edition of heaven on earth; or (to mention only one of the ideological ingredients of our time) complete pragmatic abandon to the processes of production and to human teamwork, if unceasing production seems to be the thread which holds present and future together.[14]

World views help organize and direct life. When world views clash as they do in America today, a person has to select a view that best suits his understanding of reality; otherwise, he will forever be the battlefield on which the various views struggle for hearing.

Values

A person has not only the seen and unseen world explained to him; he also has the world of social relations described to him. There is rather wide agreement in the social sciences that values are formed by the interaction of people in a historically conditioned culture. The exact definition of a value differs somewhat among the social scientists, but the definition offered by Clyde

Kluckhohn seems to have wide acceptance. "A value is a conception, explicit or implicit, distinctive of an individual or characteristic of a group, of the desirable which influences the selection from available modes, means, and ends of action."[15]

There are three main ideas in this definition. First, the word "conception." Values exist in the minds of individuals. Values are abstractions or generalizations which have been extracted from common human experience. Values are not just individual preferences such as "I like spinach"; rather, values have a built-in moral "oughtness." As Kluckhohn states it, a value "is a preference that is felt and/or considered to be justified."[16] It is what a person believes he should desire. Although values arise out of deep emotional conditioning, they are felt in the conscious mind to the extent that we believe we should act a certain way even if we are not fully aware of the reasons for the action. Specific acts are what we see and discuss, and we usually do this on the basis of whether the act will be approved or disapproved, rather than with reference to the motive or reason for the acts.

Second, the word "desirable." Values are what a person believes to be desirable, as distinct from what a person himself desires. A person has many desires based on physical need and personal wishes. A person's desires are often impulsive, based on his psychological make-up, or they are wants based on taste and habits he has developed. A person who likes baseball is expressing a personal desire, not the desirable for everybody. Values are whatever is considered proper for people in general. It is in this sense that the formulation and enactment of a public law is the practical outworking of values in society. Very often the preamble to a public law will state the values it seeks to implement. For example, the "Act for International Development of 1961" states in Section 102:

> It is the sense of the Congress that peace depends on wider recognition of the dignity and interdependence of men, and survival of free institutions in the United States can best be assured in a worldwide atmosphere of freedom.
> To this end, the United States has in the past provided assistance to help strengthen the forces of freedom by aiding peoples of

less developed friendly countries of the world to develop their resources and improve their living standards, to realize their aspirations for justice, education, dignity, and respect as individual human beings, and to establish responsible governments.[17]

Values are moral in the sense that they establish the normal patterns of behavior and that deviations from these patterns are considered wrong. However, it is incorrect to limit the expression of values to law and morals, for values underlie a whole range of judgment from the artistic to the practical way a group of people goes about its work. Kluckhohn says, "The cue words are 'right' or 'wrong,' 'better' or 'worse.' "[18] The cue words reflect an oughtness. People feel that in any situation there is a way one should act, and they either express themselves in the light of their values or they talk about the situation to find, in company with others in the same situation, what the values should be. Human life is moral because people living together have to have a knowledge of what is expected of them and what they can expect of others. Kluckhohn answers the question "Why are there values?" with these words: "Because social life would be impossible without them; the functioning of the social system could not continue to achieve group goals; individuals could not get what they want and need from other individuals in personal and emotional terms, nor could they feel within themselves a requisite measure of order and unified purpose."[19]

Third, the word "selection." Although values function through individuals in the formation of law and in the establishment of patterns of conduct in all human associations (such as business organizations, church, or labor unions), the place where we see them most clearly at work is in the ordinary lives of individuals. Whenever we see a person select a vocation, spend his money, work in a certain pattern, or use his time a certain way, we are observing the results of his values. Values are what people generally think is desirable, and what they select to do or say is the expression of their values.

We must also be clear about the relation of the individual to values. Although values are the product of culture, individuals carry and transmit values. Individuals are not automatons. They have personal preferences, and they sometimes think about the values that have been transmitted to them. There is always a private interpretation of values as well as a private awareness of values. The individual has an allegiance to the values he has received. It is also true that individuals may deliberately change some of their values or may raise their children with a different hierarchy of values from those they received from their parents.

AMERICAN VALUES

So far, we have been discussing culturally determined values as a natural function of every human group in order to establish the fact that the process of creating and transmitting values is inevitable. To see exactly how values function and the special way they are communicated it is necessary that we look at a particular culture and the history of that culture. History is an account of the past that has shaped the mind of the present generation. Although history gives stability to our inquiry concerning values, it also requires that we allow a certain amount of latitude in trying to describe values exactly, because history is not an exact science. Moreover, values change as a culture faces new situations. Any effort to formulate American values requires a certain amount of leeway in order to take account of the dynamic social situation from which they are abstracted. Reality is in the social situation, so a formulation of what is going on in that living community of thought and feeling is to some extent artificial.

Ralph H. Gabriel prepared an essay for UNESCO to introduce to India the values in American life. He listed two major values which come from our religious tradition from the Middle East: "1. The idea of the importance of the individual soul in the eyes of God. 2. The idea that Deity not only approves righteous behavior but has laid down a moral law to govern the relations of men in society."[20] Gabriel then continues to deal more specifically with American history to show the way in which specific values have developed in the areas of politics, law, religion, education, society, science, economics, the arts, and international relations. The specific values in each facet of our culture are important for full understanding of American life, and the reader is encouraged to examine

Gabriel's essay and refer to his carefully selected bibliography if he is interested in an overview of the whole American value structure. For our purposes, we would like to examine those values that are carried along in our society generally and that become the operating principles of our group life. These nine social values as presented by Gabriel are as follows:

> 1. The dignity and importance of the individual person. The individual person is, himself, a unique center of power and value. He does not exist for the state. The state, in fact, is no more than an organized community of persons. The state has no being or meaning apart from these persons. The state is an instrument to further the welfare of the persons who compose it.

This individualism is expressed in the Bill of Rights and is one of the most expensive social values to maintain. Criminals are also entitled to utilize all the features of our legal system, based on this value, in order to escape detention and prosecution. This individualism explains, in part, our political system; for we assume that if anything is wrong in the government it can be changed by changing our leaders and our policies. This individualism permeates all of our social institutions, including the church.

> 2. Freedom of thought and action of the individual person. If a person is to have dignity and if his life is to have significance, he must have a large measure of freedom. Nature, of course, sets limitations to that freedom. The prime social limitation lies in the fact that the individual person must manage his behavior so as not to impair the freedom of his fellows.

This freedom includes the religious realm, for we believe that a person should be free to worship or not worship according to the dictates of his conscience and that the state should not use any of its power to foster religious belief.

> 3. Freedom, and so far as possible equal opportunity, of the individual person to make of his life what he can in accordance with his abilities. The corollary of this concept—the expectation of a status in society that derives from his qualities and achievements.

The series of Supreme Court cases beginning with the Sweatt case in 1950 concerning desegregation of public schools has been decided on the broad principle that equality is not possible without integrating schools. The civil rights struggle which broke out in the decade of the 1960's was also based on the assumption that every person must have equal rights to vote and to enjoy every form of public accommodation.

4. Regard for the group and for group activity as a means to the ends of developing individual personality and of enlarging the possibilities for effective action that has importance for the individual person, resulting in the formation of voluntary associations in extraordinary number and for a wide range of interests.

Democracy is more than a political philosophy. It has permeated our thinking so that the collective will of the group is a powerful authority in determining what is right. Moreover, democracy as a method of solving problems has engendered the confidence that, if we can just get the right group of people to work on a problem long enough, a solution will be found.

5. Regard for the family as the basic social institution. Within the family, emphasis on the separate individualities of husband, wife, and children and the enjoyment by women of equal legal and political rights. Protection in law and custom of the privacy and mutual loyalty of its members—one spouse may not be compelled to testify in court against the other.

6. Regard for work leading to recognizable accomplishment—professional preferment, the accumulation of property—as a normal aspect of the good life. The value is expressed in the fact that having a job gives in itself a kind of social status. The tendency is to look down upon an idle man unless the idleness is due to infirmity or age. This value expresses the activism in American civilization.

Work, in short, is good, and we normally depreciate a person who achieves distinction through inheritance or luck rather than by work. We value success that can be measured in some tangible way which indicates that a person has worked hard. Success now has such high value that we have almost gotten to the place where we justify any method which brings distinction. A mass evangelist can gloss over a critical appraisal of the truth of his message if he has a crowd following him; an entertainer can be forgiven almost any personal failures, including dope addiction, if he can maintain popularity. Success has such a high value in American culture now that it is almost self-validating: any thing (or person) that is successful is good.

> 7. Concern for the physical and mental health of the community. This value emerged in the latter half of the nineteenth century when scientific advances enlarged the ability of the doctor to cure disease and made preventive medicine possible.

Out of our Judeo-Christian tradition has come a sense of charity and responsibility for persons who are victims of disease, poverty, or natural calamity such as flood or earthquake.

> 8. Regard for voluntary public service by private individuals. . . . Regard for voluntary public service implies two things. It suggests on the one hand the habit that has been developed among citizens of the United States from the wage earner to the man of wealth to make regular voluntary contributions of money to institutions and causes which further the general welfare. It implies on the other hand willingness on the part of private persons to serve without compensation in the management and promotion of such institutions and causes. The ideal of voluntary public service by private individuals ranks high in the hierarchy of American values.

This value motivates the laymen's participation in a church activity and explains the easy way Americans move between church, civic, and other volunteer organizations as they seek to actualize their community goals.

> 9. Acceptance of change as a normal aspect of social life and regard for the social sciences as instruments for gaining an understanding of society and for the formulation of improvements.

Acceptance of change is an expression of our concern for progress and improvement. We expect to develop a higher standard of living and to find new ways to do all things; changes are part of the price we must pay for keeping up any technical society.

CLASS VALUES

General social values are interpreted in special ways by each social class, and in some cases class values can all but negate general social values. Class values are communicated by the family, by the neighborhood, by work and recreation groups of people who share a common station in life and therefore a common set of interests. For our purpose, we need not catalogue special class values in detail, but it is important to note that there are significant differences in class values. Religious groups tend to be composed of people from a geographical area and reflect the class interest of the neighborhood. Therefore, in this approach to communication we must also be clear about the special class values that exist in a particular religious group as well as the general social values of the culture.

In brief, we might sketch some of the more specific class values by contrasting several classes. The professional managerial upper middle class gives a lot of attention to career, both in terms of the choice of career and of the progress one makes in his career. This class stresses the need for intelligence, drive, and adaptability to new conditions. This class is not especially interested in the past; its members are concerned about the present and the future and are anxious to be able to control both their lives and the activity around them. They accent the individual-responsibility-success value because they have achieved by sheer ability and determination; and they believe that anyone can be successful if he will just try hard enough.

The middle class, made up of people in junior managerial positions, owners of small business, office workers, and foremen, are often aware that their jobs will not move them upward any further; so they stress the respectability of their position. Education has a high value for this class; it is the main route upward to a better position and to fuller enjoyment of life. The more specific values of this class might be summed up as respect for property, social responsibility, family stability, postponement of gratification, supression of physical aggression, obedience to authority, honesty, and foresight. The twelve Boy Scout laws serve as a handy and accurate summary of middle-class values.

The lower class, which is made up of blue-collar workers, semiskilled factory workers, and unskilled clerical workers, is a stable group with little expectation of moving to higher positions. Here and there a family in this class may be able to provide opportunity for the children to get an education beyond high school and thus advance to a different class. However, in the main, members of this class are conscious of their limitations and have a sense of alienation not only from their work, which does not have much meaning in itself, but also from the community because they have neither the social skill nor the education to shape the world in which they live. Their chief satisfaction comes from their family and from recreation. Although education is known to be important, very few people of the lower class have benefited from college education and none of their friends has been helped by formal education; so children are given little encouragement to go beyond the legal age for school attendance or beyond high school.

ILLUSTRATIONS OF THE FORMATIVE POWER OF CLASS VALUES

A few illustrations of this method of analysis may be helpful at this point as a way of showing why this cultural approach must precede any other consideration in our effort to communicate the Christian faith. In our culture, where varied religious traditions have developed within a denominational pattern of church life, we can see more clearly the relation of class values to denomination than in countries where there is a state church. Richard Niebuhr's classic study, *The Social Sources of Denominationalism,*[21] shows how class interests and denominational beliefs and practices are related and how religious groups starting as sects with a lower-class clientele later became respectable middle-class denominations. But even if we had never read Niebuhr's book, we know from our own observations that sect groups are often made up of the lower classes who have been disfranchised; and we suspect that their world view (which puts so much attention on a cataclysmic end to the world and glory in heaven for all who hold to the beliefs of the sect) is in some measure a recompense for their lack of social power and acceptance in the community in which they live. Thus, the lower-class situation creates an outlook and interpretation of social values which determines in an important way the character of their Christian faith.

The middle-class situation also creates an outlook and interpretation of social values which can modify the Christian tradition. Here the problem is more subtle. The middle class is so closely allied with, and so responsible for, the secular culture that it is difficult to separate the two blending sets of values. Moreover, many of the middle-class values are the same as those of the Christian tradition. Christianity certainly teaches honesty, industry, personal responsibility, concern for others, a sense of equality whereby all men can receive justice under law, and many other values. The problem comes when we take a cultural value, such as individual success—the log-cabin-to-presidency model—and apply that to the life of Jesus as has been done in some of our curriculum material. The story of Jesus is then told as an American success story: Jesus, born in a manger, grew up to be the greatest religious leader and most successful martyr the world has ever seen! When we tell the story of Jesus in this way, we not only falsify the apostolic tradition but we also reinforce the cultural success motif; so the church becomes just another institution, like the public school, which retails the current consensus of values.

Some of the visual material we use to illustrate the Bible unconsciously puts American values in ancient Palestinian clothes. I have in my office a large picture to be used in a church school. It is designed to illustrate Samuel's anointment of Saul as leader of Israel and shows Saul toward the center of the picture on a slight hill, standing tall and erect with his right hand over his heart and his eyes to the sky. Behind him is Samuel pouring the ointment on his head, and around the two central figures are a large number of people with cheerful faces, holding their hands up in the air. Here you have clear-cut American democracy: the group gives the appearance of voting for Saul, and Saul stands with the same posture as a schoolchild who is taking the oath of allegiance to the flag. Under the picture is given the Biblical reference to 1 Samuel 9:1-3, 14-17; 10:1. If you look up those verses, including the omitted 9:27, you will be surprised to find that the anointment took place early in the morning with no witnesses, for Samuel would not even allow Saul's servant to observe the scene! Here again the Biblical message is falsified and the original idea of a charismatic king is eliminated in favor of a democratically chosen king, because in America authority for leadership is vested in the group. We know enough about Biblical tradition to refrain from using American values to interpret the Biblical stories in this fashion.

HOW CULTURE TRAINS

We have been advancing the thesis that culture forms the individual. The agencies that do the actual work of socializing are the parents or adults assigned to train the children, small primary societies, and informal work and recreation groups. We have indicated that culture transmits a world view and a set of values. These elements, because they are an explanation of the world in which we live and the world of social relations which we create, are the real forces that shape our lives; therefore, a meaningful discussion of the communication of Christian faith must keep in mind these elements of culture. By examining this natural process we are able to see why culture is so deep within us, why it is so completely a part of our emotional and intellectual make-up, and why the culture we absorb controls our interpretation of life. With this basic phenomenon in mind we shall be able in subsequent chapters to explore the problems of communicating the Christian faith.

At the beginning we must clear up a general misunderstanding of how culture is communicated and the value of this process for us. It has often been pointed out that "learning is life," or that "experience is the great teacher." This idea, expressed in various degrees of sophistication, suggests that culture is communicated as a person absorbs whatever there is around him, and that therefore authentic education is to make this process as normal and pleasant as possible. There is truth in this position. Our culture is appropriated through informal, sporadic, and spontaneous interplay of people going about their normal activity. But what is missed by this position is the deliberateness that accompanies our informal interaction and the sharp instructional activity that goes on between adults and children in every culture. A culture is anything but a helter-skelter or a you-can-do-anything-you-like proposition. Any culture that endures is deliberate in transmitting itself to the rising generation. The reason adults are so deliberate in their instruction is the realization that they will one day be dead and that the only hope they have for continuing what they consider to be good is in carefully instructed children. What may appear to be casual is actually the most powerful form of communication because it is so deliberate and so sharply directed to children by adults on whom they are dependent.

The natural agencies of instruction which form the mind of the rising generation leave a powerful guidance system within the individual. First, the process of explaining the world to a child fixes a perceptive system so that he sees the world he was instructed to see. Second, the process of training the child by rewards and punishments to think and act according to the values of his culture produces a conscience which for the rest of the person's life punishes him when he violates the code and also gives him a sense of confidence and well-being when he lives according to the values of his culture. Third, the process of coming into self-consciousness in a particular family and its primary societies develops a self-identification which colors all of his attitudes toward human relations. While the three processes are intertwined, they are distinct enough to allow us to analyze them separately.

Perceptive System

The first process is closely related to the development of a child's ability to use language. Language itself is a cultural creation and reflects in a profound way the world view of the people using the language. For example, Americans have but two words to describe the development of a coconut: "ripe" and "green," which can be modified to mean "not quite ripe" or "very green." Contrast the Marshallese, who have twelve different words to describe the stages of maturity of a coconut and over sixty words to describe the tree and its fruit. The Marshallese teach their children to identify each word with the appropriate condition of the coconut. American children could never see these different degrees of maturity unless they were equally well taught.[22] Language is, in its vocabulary and structure, a reflection of what people in a given culture have come to see and believe about the world in which they live.

As a child learns to use language, he is told the meaning of the world in which he lives, and in hundreds of ways this meaning is demonstrated for him. Kluckhohn describes how a Navaho child learns witchcraft:

> The child, even before he is fully responsive to verbalizations, begins to get a picture of experience as potentially menacing. He sees his parents, and other elders, confess their impotence to deal with various matters by technological or other rational means in that they resort to exoteric prayers, songs and "magical" observances and to esoteric rites. When he has been linguistically socialized, he hears the hushed gossip of witchcraft and learns that there are certain fellow tribesmen whom his family suspect and fear. One special experience of early childhood which may be of considerable importance occurs during toilet training. When the toddler goes with mother or with older sister to defecate or urinate, a certain uneasiness which they manifest (in most cases) about the concealment of the waste matter can hardly fail to become communicated to the child. The mother, who has been seen not only as a prime source of gratification but also as an almost omnipotent person, is now revealed as herself afraid, at the mercy of threatening forces. . . .[23]

In contrast, we can think of the average Protestant child in America who in the midst of a similar situation where the power of nature is displayed—as in an electric storm—sees his mother going about her regular work. When he asks what lightning is, he is told in a matter-of-fact tone of voice that it is a discharge of electricity from cloud to cloud; no special significance is given the event except that the child may be told how a person can protect himself in the storm. The child learns that if he takes certain precautions he has nothing to fear from nature and that nature has no claims on him.

The result of this deliberate instruction about the world results in the fixing of a perceptive system in the child which is extremely difficult to change. A person sees what he is taught to see and, seeing it, proves that it is there. Circular reasoning is built on circular seeing. The Navaho child, having been taught that there are spirits back of the world of nature, sees evidence of these spirits and relates his life to the spirits. The Protestant American child has been taught that the natural world can be explained and used, and he therefore sees nature in relationship to the problems and possibilities inherent within it.

The perceptive system also orders the world of social relations. Most of the studies that have been made in this area relate to prejudice, indicating that our socializers give us stereotypes which focus our attention on things that fit the stereotype. A classic study cited by Gordon Allport shows how the built-in perceptive system changes facts to fit a stereotype. This study was conducted by showing pictures to people who in turn explained to others what they saw; the researchers could observe the way fact shifted to fiction. One picture was of a New York subway, showing a variety of people of various races. One person in the center was a well-dressed Negro; nearby was a white person poorly dressed, with an open straight-edged razor in his hand. As people described this picture to others, they soon had the razor in the Negro's hand![24]

The perceptive system which becomes fixed in early childhood is part of the psychological make-up of each individual. The exact nature of the perceptive system has to be judged in the light of the individual's personal history, but as a phenomenon it is common to us all. Harry S. Sullivan has traced this common experience to the early years of an infant's life when he learns that some things cannot be obtained or that certain things cause extreme trouble; the child learns *not* to see or experience those things. Sullivan has labeled this situation "selective inattention," and has noted that it continues throughout a person's life.

This "suspension of awareness" is the cause of our failure to learn from certain experiences. If the experience has been pre-judged by our perceptive system, we do not see the full experience that is going on before us. We perceive only that part of the experience to which our mind has been conditioned to respond; and this familiar part of the total experience to which we respond is interpreted according to predetermined patterns.[25] Thus, a child in his most impressionable years may learn that people in authority are not to be questioned and that he must adjust his decisions to what the authority-person says. If this reaction pattern is fixed, he will probably see any authoritative person in this way and will have difficulty making independent judgments about what people in authority require him to do.

Conscience

The second process is related to conduct. A baby learns soon after he is born that there is an external authority that requires him to act a certain way. If he does not do so, he is punished; and if he does act the way the authority requires, he is rewarded. At first, the baby is required to act only in relation to feeding, later in relation to toilet training, and then, with the development of the ability to use language, the child finds that almost all of his actions have certain expectations which are governed by the adults around him. As the baby grows, he internalizes the authority within himself. Conscience is extremely moral; for, when the internalized code is violated, guilt is precipitated and the self will feel restive and ill at ease until something is done to restore the previous state of equilibrium. The guilty self will find a way to restore harmony by some psychological mechanism such as self-punishment, a denial that the action took place or that he is responsible, or a projection of guilt onto others by scapegoating. Much of this process is unconscious, because the conscience in its elementary form came into being when the person was too young to remember and because the authority was imposed on a baby by punishment. Since the conscience was formed by these nonrational means, obedience to authority is most often unconscious and is motivated by fear of guilt or punishment. Thus, a powerful regulator is implanted in a child not only in respect to authority generally but also in respect to the conduct the socializers approve or disapprove. In this sense, Durkheim is profoundly right in saying, "Everything that is found in conscience comes from society." A study of a variety of cultures will show that a person can be conditioned to accept almost any kind of behavior as right.

Although the negative side of conscience—those things we must not do—is deep within our person and rests only partly in our conscious mind, there is also a positive side to conscience. As a child is socialized, he voluntarily accepts many of the patterns of action and principles of living which are displayed to him by his parents and the adults around him. These things become more a part of his conscious mind because they develop later as the result of a positive identification with the adults who guided him. The child may literally want to be a helpful person because he likes the helpful quality in his parents and willingly incorporates this trait within himself. When a person violates his positive conscience, he experiences shame because he has broken the code of conduct that he has voluntarily accepted; this causes a reflective, introspective dialogue within himself, with questions such as these: "Why did I do that? What can I do to avoid that in the future? How can I make restitution?" Shame forces us to face our understanding of what we want to be, and as such it is related to the identification we have with our parents and the adults in the primary societies through which we formed our self-image. In short, we feel proud when we have lived up to what we believe we ought to be and are self-confident that the groups which mean most to us will approve our actions.[26]

Self-Identification

The third process is related to the primary social group to which the child is related. A person comes into self-understanding only in relation to others in his immediate environment. This identification of a person's selfhood with a group will be a lasting feature of his life. He may, of course, seek to change his self-identification. The socially mobile person who seeks to move from a laboring-class home background to a middle-class professional status is a fairly common illustration. However, to be successful the mobile person has to learn the style of life of his new group identity. It is difficult to imagine life without reference to a group to which a person attaches his self-understanding. The group does not always have to be physically present, nor does the group have to have clearly defined behavioral patterns for all conceivable situations. A person can refer to his group mentally and imagine how his group would expect him to act in the concrete circumstances he faces.[27]

There are two things in this process which we need to observe. First, as a child grows up, practically every situation he encounters is new; but seldom is the situation new to the group. There is an accumulated wisdom stored in the group's corporate memory which is told to the children. Often this wisdom or knowledge about situations is told to the child directly about concrete situations—how to behave before old people, how to save money for future use, and so on. Much of this instruction is about things that do not happen, such as our warning to girls never to accept a ride from a strange man or what to do if a child is hurt and cannot get in touch with the parents. This special and direct instruction related to the specific social group to which the child belongs can even be factually wrong and yet be carried along for generations without correction. For example, the knowledge that the world is round was known by educated Europeans for generations before it was accepted by the masses. A common fact that vegetables need very little cooking and can have some of their nourishment removed by too much cooking is ignored by millions of housewives who cook vegetables as they were taught to cook them in their parents' home. Social facts are even more stubbornly related to group beliefs. The fact that no race is naturally inferior to another is not accepted by millions of people in many countries of the world because they were carefully taught by their social group that certain races are inferior. Classroom instruction to the contrary is relatively weak in the face of group-induced attitudes.[28]

Second, the method of appropriating the group pattern of behavior or style of life is done more through imitation than through any other method. The child is in a situation where, compared to adults, he is weak and ignorant and without experience by which he can make independent judgments. Therefore, at an early age he learns to imitate adults. The adults who nurture children usually show them how to act or tell them what to think or say. This coaching is so successful that the child learns not only how to act but also how to depend on adults. The adults with whom he gets along well become for him powerful models for imitation. This process of ego-identity is easiest to observe when the child is two or three years old and models himself according to the superior adults—usually his parents. In early adolescence when the usefulness of the parent-figure is waning, the child develops a "crush" on adults in the immediate community who personify the characteristics he wants to acquire. Many adolescents make their vocational choice not on the basis of their native ability but on the basis of the vocation of some adult who at this crucial time in their self-development becomes their ideal.

Imitation is the method by which a person appropriates the style of life of the group in which he comes into selfhood, whether that group is a criminal gang, a Protestant sect, a conservative Jewish subculture, or a suburban neighborhood. The style of life is a set of behavioral patterns by which specific life situations are met and handled. Although a person indulges in a certain amount of trial-and-error behavior on his own, most of his habits are formed by imitating the older people in the family and small social groups to which he belongs.

The self, then, is in large measure an extension of the nurturing group. A person most often accepts the value of his self which others assign to him. One of the tragedies of the racial conflict in America is the knowledge that many Negroes have internalized the value of their self that white people assigned them. Social scientists have long been aware that a Negro child had to learn to be a Negro and that a negative self-identification prevented him from asserting himself.[29] The current civil rights movement is more a desire for self-respect and a demand for treatment that will foster self-respect than it is for any specific social goal.

The lower-class adolescent, especially the boy, finds on every hand people who assume that he will be a laborer or semiskilled worker and will not finish or go beyond high school. Unfortunately, the average public high school through its teachers and class situation reinforces this attitude, and in most cases the lower-class adolescent incorporates it as a part of his self-identity. Acting on what he has accepted, he drops out of school and settles for that kind of life.[30]

CULTURE AND COMMUNICATION

This brief discussion of culture defines our approach to the problem of communicating the Christian faith. We start with culture because it supplies—along with other things—a world view and a set of values, and Christianity attempts to do that, too. We start with culture because it communicates its beliefs by a natural process which molds society, informal groups, and the individual, a process that Christianity could use for the same purpose.

We also start with culture because it is a reality we know.

Christianity is a part of our culture and is, we hope, capable of being somewhat apart from our culture. Since culture is always related to a group of people, this approach is a radical, historical one. It is not radical in the sense of being iconoclastic but in the true meaning of radical—going to the root of the matter, which is the assumption that we must know the history of a people to know their culture. History is what people think is worth remembering and passing on, so we have in history our source of a people's world view and values and their appraisal of what must be passed on in order to secure the future they think desirable.

III

The Dynamics of Religious Tradition

Our discussion has focused on culture in order to understand the way human beings order their lives in groups. We found that three training processes were at work incessantly in a wide variety of relationships and that each process left a powerful mechanism within the individual which made him an agent for transmitting what was given to him. Although this analysis is helpful in understanding the process of socialization, culture itself is always historical because it relates to a particular people living at a certain time and in a certain place. Since our interest is in Western culture, specifically that of America, we shall confine ourselves to the problem of communicating the Christian faith within this culture and from the standpoint of our Protestant tradition.

At once, we are confronted with the problem of pluralism. American culture is made up of many religious groups. Although these religious groups hold important social values in common, they also preserve their particular world view, values, and ceremonies. In order to reserve the word "culture" for the total society, we shall use the word "tradition" in referring to a religious group. The "tradition" of a religious group indicates its distinctive style of life through a historical period; for example, the Calvinist, Lutheran, or Baptist tradition. These religious traditions function as subcultures in our pluralistic Western society. It is our thesis that the general process of socialization described in the last chapter operates within each religious tradition and that our efforts to communicate the Christian faith should be planned to use these natural and powerful processes more deliberately.

TRADITION AS TRANSMISSION

To be religious one has to be in a certain tradition. All religions have individuals who are innovators modifying the tradition given to them or reformers who drastically change a belief system; and occasionally a charismatic leader appears who develops a new religion. But in all of these cases the work of the leader is established and maintained by a group of believers who are able to systematize the insights and affirmations of the leader into a historical tradition. However, traditions are not created out of thin air; they are historically rooted in men, movements, and events which, in turn, are historically conditioned.

This view is so widespread that we hardly realize how modern it is or how many problems it poses. "For modern man," Gerhard Ebeling writes, "everything, the whole of reality, turns to history."[1] Ebeling continues, "Never in the whole history of theology up to modern times was there such a thing as taking a historical view of a theological problem."[2] Thinkers have always been aware of the past and have used the thoughts and historical events of the past in their work, yet they did so on the assumption that they could establish generalized statements of truth which would endure. St. Augustine did indeed set the main outline of thought that endured for a thousand years in Western civilization, and the Protestant Reformers did establish guidelines for a system of theology that has endured for four hundred years; but we interpret each of these systems of theology in relation to the conditions that produced it and we expect succeeding generations to interpret our thought in relation to our culture.

We Protestants have serious intellectual and emotional difficulties in bringing our religious beliefs into harmony with our modern historical knowledge. A standard Protestant version of the past affirms that there was a clear revelation from God, verbally correct, which resided within the New Testament church. Early believers—guided by the Holy Spirit—struggled against Roman authority and against Jewish and Greek cultures and finally, through perseverance and persecution, became the true church. Although it remained relatively pure for a while, this church eventually became corrupt because of arrogant leaders and the slow accretion of non-Biblical doctrines; but after the Reformation the New Testament church was once more established. This oversimplified summary reveals two assumptions scholars have now proven false. We now know that the New Testament itself is a collection of historical documents each of which has to be analyzed in order to find the apostolic message within it; and, when that message is found, it has to be interpreted in the light of the ideas and events of the historical situation that produced it. We also know that the Reformers were not free to stand outside their cultural inheritance and re-establish a New Testament church. They, too, were creatures of culture and must be judged on the basis of the conditions they met and the conditions they created by their actions and by their theology.

The connection between past and present in religion is tradition. That is a reality with which we must deal. It is extremely unfortunate that the word "tradition" to most Protestants connotes conservatism—the dead hand of the past controlling the present. Albert Outler has said:

> It is ironic, and rather sad, that the word "tradition" has come in modern times to connote stagnation and resistance to an open future. In common parlance "traditional" and "modern" are actually antonyms. We need, therefore, to recall that the root meaning of "tradition" is active and transitive. Tradition denotes *an act*— the handing over of something from the past to the future. It serves the double purpose of salvaging that past from oblivion and of furnishing the future with ballast. No community can persist for as long as three generations without vital traditions and effective traditioners. Just as amnesia can blot out an individual's self-awareness (and, in so doing, wreak psychic havoc) so also, the lapse of the traditionary process can distintegrate and demoralize a society with shocking speed. More than once now, modern man has seen this very thing happen before his very eyes.[3]

Outler's definition uses tradition as the connection between past and present. He correctly puts his finger on the transmission process as an act sponsored by traditioners in a "traditionary" process, which we can equate with the socializing process described in the preceding chapter. The matter stated in these terms helps us see clearly that the issue is not whether we will accept tradition as reality; the only issue is what tradition we will transmit through the hundreds of "acts" in which we are engaged every day. To say that we Protestants are against all tradition and live only by the Bible is to select an "anti-tradition" tradition which goes back to the Reformation and which has been reinforced by native American individualism. We must constantly remind ourselves that a tradition is whatever we transmit. In that sense a tradition can be conservative or liberal; it can resist change or open a person to expect change.

TRADITION AND THE BIBLE

The modern understanding of history to which we referred earlier tends to relativize everything, including the present. We not only see the past in relation to the historical circumstances that made it, but we also see ourselves conditioned by forces, circumstances, and ideas that we must handle our own way, knowing that the next generation will have to meet different circumstances and order its life its own way. This raises the question of relativity to the order of truth, and many are asking if there is anything significant about the Christian faith. Was the Christian faith a development in the history of religions that is now passing? Are we entering an age when mature men can live without religion? There is no answer that can be given to this question which will satisfy the skeptics, for the skeptic mind will not accept any of the arguments that can be advanced in favor of the Christian faith. The only answer that has any meaning today is the answer that is lived. The only choice for Christians is to be true to the Christian tradition, to reinterpret the symbols of their faith as best as they can in their day. Our descendants will be able to give a word of judgment about the truth of our claim in the light of what we make of our lives in relation to the problems we face; they can compare our solutions with those produced by other religions and other cultures. The final test for the claim of the truth in a religious tradition is time.[4]

This does not mean that we have abandoned the search for truth or that truth about God is not available from the past. The Bible is the definitive source for a description of the God in whom we have faith, though we do not expect the Bible to answer all of our questions about modern life. Although we are required to make judgments about the past, this does not mean that we are adrift on an ocean of opinion. It means that the effort to find certainty in the past is a misguided one; we have to find our faith in the God who is present to us today as he was present to believers in the past. What God means for us today will be significantly related to the conditions we face, just as God was significantly related to the events and conditions our predecessors faced.

When we ask of the Bible "What is this book?" rather than "What truth does this book contain?" our attention is focused on the unique relation of the Bible to a tradition that has existed for at least four thousand years; we begin to see the way a people who had faith in God were formed by tradition, how they reformed tradition in the light of new revelation, and how they were able to carry along in a stream of history various points of view about God. Tradition overrides a logically worked-out belief system. The Bible is a paradox. It describes God's revelation as being conditioned by the mentality of the people who received it, yet that revelation from God changed the nature of the people's self-understanding and of their historical destiny.

We have a Bible because faith in God is communal. The community of believers, both in the Old and New Testaments, came first, and their written record of that faith came into existence later. The writings were, without exception, produced for corporate worship or to teach, exhort, guide, warn, judge, inspire, or regulate by law (and morals) the life of a believing community. God was in the tradition—that is, in the events that came to be recorded—and these events were recorded because the community of believers believed that God was active in their history. The record itself was not sacred; it was a description of their history which had become sacred to them. The books of the Bible are all intimately related to the faith of a community of believers who put their stories, songs, historical narratives, and creeds in written form in order to preserve the meaning of faith for themselves and their children.

New Testament

To be more specific, let us look at the way the Christian Bible came into being. Jesus left no written record. All that we know about him is contained in books that were written years after his death, and these books were not at the beginning considered the authoritative source of knowledge about him. If we examine this process of development in broad outline, we will better understand the role of the Bible in relation to faith; and we will also gain an understanding of the natural communication process that is inherent in a living tradition.

The first group of writings in the New Testament is by the Apostle Paul, starting about A.D. 48 with his letter to the Thessalonians and concluding at his death about A.D. 67. The church was already a going concern when Paul's first letter appeared; we know from his writings that the believers observed the sacraments, had a pattern of local church organization, had well-developed ethical practices, missionary activity, and a style of worship. All of Paul's letters were written to specific churches, and there is no reason to believe his letters were intended for general circulation. However, we know that they were published as a group by A.D. 100 and were in general use in the churches after that date.

The second group of writings is the Synoptic Gospels and Acts, which came into existence between about A.D. 70 and 90. Each of these books was composed largely of oral traditions which had been handed down, plus the sayings of Jesus which had probably been collected and were in general circulation in various forms. Different communities of believers using these materials over a period of time shaped them into books; but there is no doubt that the oral tradition about the meaning of the life, death, and resurrection of Jesus was the central data and dynamic that formed these books. Mark's Gospel probably came from a community of believers at Rome; Matthew's came from a community of believers in Palestine; and Luke's from a community in the Eastern Mediterranean. It is important to observe that no one of these Gospels was prepared to supplement the other; each Gospel was related to the needs and problems of a specific community of believers.

The third group of writings, the pastoral epistles and the Revelation, was produced between about A.D. 95 and 150. A reading of any of these books in comparison to the letters of Paul will show that Christians in this later period were concerned with stabilizing the church, conserving the apostolic tradition, and interpreting the gospel to meet new conditions. In many of these books we find an admonition for the people to "follow the pattern of the sound words which you have heard from me" (2 Timothy 1:13). This oral tradition ("sound words") was to be passed on by teaching to others (2 Timothy 2:2). Authority in the church had become vested in elders or bishops, who at this stage, incidentally, were not in charge of a diocese but of a local congregation. "Bishop" and "presbyter" were synonyms for the pastoral office at this point in the church's history; the authority of these leaders was derived from their connection through earlier presbyters to eyewitnesses of Christ's resurrection, showing that authority was not invested in the office but in one's connection with the resurrection of Christ and with Christ's ministry prior to his crucifixion.

It is important to note that all through this period the books which make up our New Testament were not considered the principal authority for a correct understanding of the Christian faith. The principal authority was the oral tradition that went back to an eyewitness of the resurrection. The Christian message in sermon, personal testimony, and training manuals was mainly an explanation of the Old Testament in the light of the words, deeds, and resurrection of Jesus Christ. An illustration of how the oral tradition about Jesus was used to interpret the Scriptures of the Old Testament is given in the book of Acts in the story of Philip and the Ethiopian eunuch. You will recall that the Ethiopian was reading from the prophet Isaiah when Philip asked him if he understood what he was reading. The Ethiopian asked for guidance; "then Philip opened his mouth, and beginning with this scripture he told him the good news of Jesus." The Ethiopian made his confession of faith in Jesus as the fulfillment of the Old Testament Scripture and was baptized (Acts 8:26-40).

It is difficult for us today to understand the power of the oral tradition. We assume that a correct statement is one that is written and can be verified, which causes us to treat oral statements as rumor or as being so highly personal in character that they cannot have general validity. This is because we live in an era that has hundreds of years of printing behind it and because all of the important things in our life—laws, records, contracts, learning— come to us in printed form. To the mind of the first century, the reverse was true. Writing, although widespread, was not the chief means of communicating important matters. For example, in the Epistle of John we read: "I have much to write to you, but I do not care to put it down in black and white. But I hope to visit you and talk with you face to face, so that our joy may be complete" (2 John 12, N.E.B.; see also 3 John 13-14). We also see this illustrated by Papias, Bishop of Hierapolis, about A.D. 135; although he had before him the Gospels according to Mark, Matthew, and John and perhaps other lives of Jesus which are now lost, he did not put his confidence in these written records but rather said:

> Unlike most people, I felt at home not with those who had a great deal to say, but with those who taught the truth; not with those who appeal to commandments from other sources but with those who appeal to the commandments given by the Lord to faith and coming to us from truth itself. And whenever anyone came who had been a follower of the presbyters, I inquired into the words of the presbyters, what Andrew or Peter had said, or Philip or Thomas or James or John or Matthew, or any other disciple of the Lord, and what Aristion and the presbyter John, disciples of the Lord, were still saying. For I did not imagine that things out of books would help me as much as the utterances of a living and abiding voice.[5]

This living, oral tradition is illustrated in the way the Gospels are related to each other. Matthew uses almost all of Mark; Luke uses Mark and other sources and begins his Gospel with these words: ". . . many have undertaken to compile a narrative of the things which have been accomplished among us, just as they were delivered to us by those who from the beginning were eyewitnesses and ministers of the word" (Luke 1:1-2). Here we see that the oral tradition has authority because it goes straight back to the eyewitnesses. We also see that there were many accounts of the life and sayings of Jesus and that Luke planned to give a more orderly, or historical, account. When we compare the Gospels, we find that none of them regards the others as definitive. They revise, modify, add, subtract, and even change the order of events in Jesus' life so that it is difficult, if not impossible, to reconstruct the chronology of his ministry. The Gospel according to John makes no effort to follow the general outline of the life of Jesus which is found in the other Gospels; John approaches the whole oral tradition in a bold and fresh way so that Jesus becomes the Word of God from the beginning of time (John 1:1-17).

From its formation soon after the resurrection to A.D. 150, the church lived by a tradition which was expressed early and clearly by Paul in 1 Corinthians 15:3-5 in these words: "For I delivered to you as of first importance what I also received, that Christ died for our sins in accordance with the scriptures, that he was buried, that he was raised on the third day in accordance with the scriptures, and that he appeared to Cephas, then to the twelve."

It was not until Marcion appeared about A.D. 150 that the church began to think seriously about which writings gave the authentic tradition. Marcion believed that the God of the Old Testament was crude and cruel and that Jesus revealed a different God of love; therefore, Marcion wanted to abandon the Old Testament entirely. In order to carry his theological point, he edited a gospel of Luke and certain letters of Paul to suit his theological beliefs and set forth his collection of writings as representing the true Christian faith. Because Marcion had eliminated the Old Testament and had emasculated the known oral tradition about Jesus, the Christian church excommunicated him for heresy. The church, however, partly in reaction to Marcion's collection of writings and partly because of the church's need to establish the true tradition, began to gather together the books which conformed to the apostolic traditions.

We can see the whole matter rather clearly in the works of Irenaeus, who wrote during the last quarter of the second century. He is important for our purposes because he was the first Christian writer to work with the Old and the New Testaments just as we do; in his writings he referred to all of the books in the New Testament except Philemon, Third John, and Jude, showing that all of the books now in the New Testament had already become normative for the work and worship of the church. Irenaeus had a sense of tradition. In his writings against heretics he appealed to "that tradition which has come down from the apostles and is guarded by the successions of elders in the churches."[6] Notice that the authentic apostolic tradition had been transmitted through elders who functioned both as teachers and leaders. Later on, Irenaeus mentions Polycarp, whom he knew as a youth, saying that Polycarp "was taught by apostles, and associated with many who had seen Christ"; he then adds that Polycarp "departed this life in a ripe old age by a glorious and magnificent martyrdom."[7]

Polycarp, therefore, was classified as an authority on what had happened because he had been with the Apostles and, by giving his life for the cause, he had certified that the truth he offered could be trusted. One paragraph from Irenaeus will show the relation between the living tradition and the written records which characterizes the Christian church in the last half of the second century.

For we learned the plan of our salvation from no others than from those through whom the gospel came to us. They first preached it abroad, and then later by the will of God handed it down to us in Writings, to be the foundation and pillar of our faith. For it is not right to say that they preached before they had come to perfect knowledge, as some dare to say, boasting that they are the correctors of the apostles. For after our Lord had risen from the dead, and they were clothed with the power from on high when the Holy Spirit came upon them, they were filled with all things and had perfect knowledge. They went out to the ends of the earth, preaching the good things that come to us from God, and proclaiming peace from heaven to men, all in each of them equally being in possession of the gospel of God. So Matthew among the Hebrews issued a Writing of the gospel in their own tongue, while Peter and Paul were preaching the gospel at Rome and founding the Church. After their decease Mark, the disciple and interpreter of Peter, also handed down to us in writing what Peter had preached. Then Luke, the follower of Paul, recorded in a book the gospel as it was preached by him. Finally John, the disciple of the Lord, who had also lain on his breast, himself published the Gospel, while he was residing at Ephesus in Asia. All of these handed down to us that there is one God, maker of heaven and earth, proclaimed by the Law and the Prophets, and one Christ the Son of God. If anyone does not agree with them he despises the companions of the Lord, he despises Christ the Lord himself, he even despises the Father, and he is self-condemned, resisting and refusing his own salvation, as all the heretics do.[8]

In that paragraph we see that the real power of the gospel is in the resurrection of Jesus Christ, that authority to explain and communicate it is in the lives of those who experienced that event, and that certain writings give an authoritative account of what happened.

The writings that formed an authoritative account of the living tradition were in general use throughout all parts of the church by the year A.D. 200, although the list of books was not precisely the same as we now have in the New Testament. Origen, who succeeded Clement as head of the school in Alexandria in the year 203, treats both the Old Testament and the New Testament books as Scripture, giving equal authority to both Testaments.

The church continued to sift the various other writings that appeared in the first one hundred fifty years of the church; and at the Third Council of Carthage in 393, it formulated an official list which settled the New Testament canon for the Western church. The Bible did not form the church, nor did the church through its tradition create the Bible. Rather, God's action in Jesus Christ— his life, death, and resurrection—formed the church as a body of believers; and the New Testament writings came into being as an authentic record of what God had done, in order that the apostolic tradition would be available to succeeding generations.

Old Testament

The story of the formation of the Old Testament is too complex to summarize briefly. Any standard dictionary of the Bible will contain an article on the Old Testament canon and recent commentaries. The reader will probably be impressed by the long time span between the first book as it now is in our Old Testament and the last book, a period of approximately 1000 years. Moreover, the material in the oldest books in the Old Testament describes events that took place at the Exodus, which is even further back in time; the stories of the patriarchs and the calling of Abraham in Genesis push the story back perhaps a thousand years before the book which now gives us the story.

The process by which the Old Testament was put into writing is the same process that we described for the New Testament. First, there was the group of believers who handed down to succeeding generations stories of God's activity among them. The people's faith was the dynamic energy that charged the stories with power, and the stories came to be written to preserve their power. When the material was written down, there was no effort to "correlate" or "correct" the stories or to make one story consistent with the next. For example, the editor of Genesis combines two stories of creation, the Priestly tradition (Genesis 1:1—2:4a) and the Yahwistic tradition (Genesis 2:4b—2:25).[9] In the narrative sections of the Old Testament there are clear contradictions, such as the numbering of the people of Israel in Judah, found in 2 Samuel 24 and in 1 Chronicles 21. Not only is the number of the people recorded differently, but the reason for the numbering is assigned to the Lord in the Samuel account and to Satan in the Chronicles account.

This phenomenon of carrying along contradictions within the stream of tradition is natural to the process and explains why it is difficult to get a consistent idea of God from the Bible. God in the Bible has many facets. There are sections in the Old Testament which make God vindictive (see Psalm 137:7-9; Judges 5:2-31), yet we have Proverbs 25:21 which says, "If your enemy is hungry, give him bread to eat" (see also Romans 12:20). Throughout the Bible we have the general assumption that God is good and that he is all-powerful, yet we have the contradiction that evil exists in spite of these characteristics of God. It is to the glory of the book of Job that this inconsistency is met head-on; yet it is not resolved, for there is no logical solution. The living stream of tradition can carry along these problems and inconsistencies without solutions just as individuals can carry along in their lives problems they are not able to solve.

The important thing in all of this is the power of the living tradition. It was not until 621 B.C. that the Book of the Law

(Deuteronomy) was officially recognized as Scripture in Israel and not until A.D. 90 that the canon of the Old Testament was officially defined as we now have it. In Israel faith was transmitted by a community, and the formulation of the account of their tradition developed over a long period of time.[10] Or, to state the matter somewhat differently, the believing community both in the Old and the New Testaments authenticated the writings that formed their tradition in order that the writings might capture in words the meaning of the revelations that had formed their tradition.

ELEMENTS IN THE BIBLICAL TRADITION

There are two elements in the Biblical tradition: the tradition that is handed down and the experience that individuals and groups have as they live, modify, and pass on the tradition. We can look back to the Old Testament and see how the religious experience of Amos and other prophets changed the tradition. But it is impossible to work out a formula that we can apply today because we do not know exactly what happened in the past. However, even if we did know, it would not necessarily happen that way again. God's Spirit is free to work out his purpose, and we cannot predict how or through whom God will act. We can, however, find some guidance for our situation today by examining the way in which the Bible reports the intermingling of tradition and experience; this will alert us to the characteristic way God leads his people to form anew the tradition that formed them.

The Luke-Acts narratives are the first major break in the New Testament away from the eschatological belief of the primitive church, which was clearly stated in Paul's letters—that Jesus would soon return to judge and rule the world. Luke-Acts was written in part to help the church settle down to live by its tradition. Even though hope for an early return of Jesus was not abandoned, still he had not returned and the church could no longer put off decisions or temporize about its problems. The church had to change its strategy of waiting for the return of Jesus to a strategy of stabilizing the messianic societies through a self-conscious explanation of their role in the world and their relation to the Jews and to other religions. Luke makes this clear when he says in his introduction that he is going to write an orderly account (1:3). This approach is continued in Acts where Jesus is quoted as saying in his last post-resurrection appearance that it is not for men to know when God will restore Israel (1:7) but that the believers are to receive the Holy Spirit and spread the gospel to the end of the earth (1:8). After these words, Jesus disappears in a cloud and the disciples retire to the upper room, where they select a replacement for Judas, move into the Pentecost experience, and then go out into the world to establish the church.[11]

It is significant that within the book of Acts believers in Christ were first called followers of "the Way." That is, Christianity was a way of life and an explanation of life combined in a human community. The word "Christian" as a descriptive noun is used only three times in the New Testament, whereas the idea of "the Way" or "following the Way" of Christ is used many times. Saul, in order to persecute Christians legally, obtained a letter from the high priest authorizing him to arrest followers of "the Way" (Acts 9:2); and toward the end of his life when he made his defense before Felix, he said, "According to the Way, which they call a sect, I worship the God of our fathers . . ." (Acts 24:14). In this sentence we have a perfect example of the role of revelation and tradition. The God of his fathers was the tradition of Israel, but in that tradition Paul was shown a new way of life.

Tradition in Experience

Tradition preceded Scripture.[12] When the Biblical revelation did come, it was always indelibly colored by the tradition into which the receiver of revelation was born. Many scholars have shown that much of what Jesus said was either from the Old Testament or was current in the Judaism of the first century. It is difficult, if not impossible, to claim that the uniqueness of Jesus lay in his teachings. The only glimpse we have of his childhood indicates that he was absorbing and evaluating the Jewish tradition as explained by the teachers in the Temple (Luke 2:41-52). According to the Gospel accounts of the life of our Lord, it was not until his baptism that he launched out on his own as the preacher and teacher of the Kingdom of God. Matthew's account of the Sermon on the Mount has Jesus constantly using the formula, "You have heard that it was said to the men of old . . . But I say to you . . ."; this indicates that he started his teaching with Judaism, the reality that was deepest and dearest to himself and his audience.

Although the Apostle Paul took as his special mission the conversion of the Gentiles, he never repudiated the Old Testament or Judaism. To the contrary, his conversion as described in Acts (9:1-22) was from Judaism to Christ, and he interpreted Christ as the fulfillment of Old Testament tradition rather than as the author of a new religion. One of Paul's first recorded sermons to a Jewish audience traces the history of Israel from the Exodus straight to Jesus (Acts 13:16-42); and at the end of his life when he had to explain and defend his conduct to the Jews (Acts 22:1-21) or to the Roman authorities (Acts 26:2-23), he always identified himself as a strict Jew and an educated Pharisee who understood and appreciated the Jewish Torah. Paul as he worked out his Christian theology had to face the Jewish tradition that was within him. When standing before a Jewish audience, he started with the tradition that motivated their lives. The amazing thing about the Apostle Paul is that he did not make the Jewish tradition normative for non-Jews as the Judaizing party sought to do by insisting that a Gentile had first to become a Jew before he could become a Christian (Acts 15). Rather, Paul started with the tradition in which the Gentile was raised, as shown by his famous sermon to the Greeks on Mars Hill (Acts 17:22-31); then he talked to the Greeks about the revelation of God in Jesus Christ.[13]

Revelation by its very nature causes a person to transcend himself, to stand outside the culture that shaped him, so that he can see himself and all of life differently. Such an experience heightens a person's awareness of the tradition in which he lives and of the changes that must be made to bring human life more in line with God's will. In fact, revelation would have no substantive meaning if it did not cause a person to evaluate the cultural matrix in which he lives; therefore, part of a revelation experience is a disclosure of the real significance of one's tradition. Revelation means much more than a critical evaluation of this tradition, but it cannot mean anything until it first brings the person to terms with the forces which have shaped his life and which continue to shape the destiny of the people with whom he lives.

We hear it said that a man is the child of his culture and we must judge his actions on the basis of the cultural situation at the time he lived. That rule is obvious. I am pointing out that revelation from God as it is described in the Bible is a radical experience that causes a person to see and understand the social forces which have shaped his life. Moreover, the revelatory experience relates a person to the cultural factors in his own life, so that part of his struggle for freedom to be what God calls him to be is with the tradition that formed his selfhood.[14]

Tradition also has precedence in our lives—not just in time, but in our understanding of life. We have to make a hundred little decisions every day on the basis of criteria that are "good" to our way of thinking. When we have to make big decisions related to vocation, marriage, or child training, we search for that which is most real in our lives so that the decision will be "right." But where did this "good" and "right" come from? It comes from the tradition in which we were nurtured.

However, we face a strange dilemma. If we rivet our tradition too tightly on our children, they will tend to follow it compulsively rather than being free to evaluate it and modify it when they become adults. As parents and teachers in the church we need to transmit our morality with kindness and firmness so that the growing child will be clear about himself and the outside world; then he will be free enough when he becomes adolescent to be able to examine critically that which was given to him. But regardless of how it happens for the particular child, the human environment is "given" and he experiences what is given to him through the adults who nurture him.

Again, I am trying to say more than the fact that we learn a specific tradition as we grow up. I am indicating that what we learn takes on the character of being "good" and "right." What we learn as children becomes an unargued assumption and, until challenged, remains the effective basis on which we build our lives. Moreover, the way we learn our heritage—by rewards and punishments—gives it a moral connotation which continues throughout our life, so that even in our mature years if we go counter to

our early experience we feel guilty or have a vague, undifferenti-
ated feeling of internal unrest. I am also saying that a baby does
not find life full of experiences out of which he develops meaning
as he matures. Rather, life is presented to the baby already structured in form and in meaning; his experiences are not his own but
are predetermined by his tradition. When the experience comes, it
is uniquely his own, but the meaning is already supplied.

It is this repertoire of culturally supplied meanings that a person
sees clearly within himself when he has a revelatory experience,
because revelation has no meaning apart from the substance of
life. Therefore, revelatory experience is never separate from tradition but is in—and over against—tradition. The Biblical model of
a person who has seen God is one who has to re-form his self. He
must re-form his self-concept in the light of the experience he has
had with God. In Christian theology a person who has experienced
Jesus Christ as Lord and Savior has a transforming experience
which slowly brings a new self into being. This new self is not cut
out of a preconceived pattern but is formed against the background of the tradition that nurtured the person. Having a conversion experience shatters one's deepest memories and dearest internal possessions in order to rebuild one's life more consciously
about a different center and toward a different goal.

I have been saying that we must start with tradition, not because
it is more important than revelation but because it is a basic
human reality which is experienced and appropriated long before a
person has the intellectual and emotional capacity to evaluate
critically or modify his tradition. This process of incorporating
tradition is probably the reason why human society is normally
conservative and why significant changes in human life come about
slowly. The experience of Moses in leading the Israelites out of
Egypt illustrates the matter perfectly. The generation of adults that
came through those experiences with him was never able to shake
off completely their slave mentality. They preferred the certainty
of food as slaves to the uncertainty and hunger in their struggle for
freedom (Exodus 16:3). Moses had to spend forty years raising a
new generation that did not have the tradition of slavery in their
bones before he could move into the promised land.

Experience in Tradition

The mental process by which we know God may not be, and probably is not, different from other kinds of knowing; but the object of our knowing—God—is different and therefore the result of such an experience is different. Revelation is an experience which changes the receiver and his total outlook on life. The experience is so real and so powerful that it becomes the center of his life, and both his past and his future are seen in the light of that experience.

Revelation from God is not the result of speculative intelligence. God did not set forth a series of ideas about himself nor did he seek to prove his existence. Rather, he elected to show himself to men through the events that made up their communal life. The Bible is a description of these events; and although we might call them "holy" because they communicated the meaning of God for the life of his people, the events themselves are not "special." To others who lived at the same time, the events were often quite ordinary, but to the person who was God's chosen interpreter the events were charged with special meaning.

This major affirmation about God—that he communicates with men through events which take place in the stream of historical tradition—puts the personal experience of revelation in its proper perspective. First, it is not a personal experience that is to be enjoyed, nor is it an experience of the holy in itself, nor is it the self-giving of God to a human self as humans give themselves to each other; rather, it is a personal awareness of what God wants the person to be and do in relation to specific situations that exist in the community in which he lives. Such a personal experience with God is different from religious experience that is generated by personal needs or psychological conditions.

Second, authentic experience with the God of the Bible is something that comes to the person from outside himself, and he is conscious that the origin of it is separate from his own being. This makes revelation sharply different from discovery, a process wherein the discoverer is conscious of his role in finding truth. Much Biblical interpretation in the immediate past has been done

on the basis of the idea of progress. It was assumed that everything human had an origin that was simple, childlike, and primitive. The Old Testament was, in its oldest part, thought to be a
religion of animism which progressively was refined through
polytheism to the highest ethical monotheism of the eighth-century
prophets and culminated in the life and teachings of Jesus. This is
true to some extent, but it is certainly not the main truth of the
Bible. It would be more accurate to say that there is development
in the Bible in the sense that one custom emerges out of a previous
one, or that one teacher used the experiences of his predecessor in
his message; but the nineteenth-century notion of progress—that
conditions are getting better—is not native to the Bible. Such a
notion of progress eliminates revelation in the Biblical sense (that
God shows men his will for particular human conditions) and
substitutes the idea that men in each stage of growing self-consciousness discover the general insights about life which accrue for
that particular stage. This assumption puts the emphasis on man's
ability to discover general religious and moral truth rather than on
God's activity in showing men his will; and such an assumption
makes God little more than a symbol for man's generalizations
about the world rather than a divine will that the people must obey
or disobey.

Third, Biblical revelation defines the area in which one has his
experiences with God. Revelation is not a grasping of the meaning
of the objects of the physical world or the realm of nature, although these things may be important as a part of a revelation
from God. These objects are part of the world and give life its
scope and limitations. Moreover, the nonhuman world has a
rhythm of its own as seen in the seasons and a power of its own as
seen in storms, volcanoes, and avalanches which impinge on the
human world. But from the Biblical view these things are not the
sources of God's revelation. That is why the Hebrews in the Old
Testament did not accept nature or fertility gods, resisted astrol-
ogy, and constantly refused to accept guidance for practical decisions from sorcerers or diviners who worked by magic. Rather,
revelation was given in a human experience which was situational.
It was concerned about human conditions in which the people

lived. The crucial factor in the definition of the Biblical experience of revelation was the need for making a decision, for casting one's life one way or another for the future. This condition of having to act in the light of particular circumstances is what sharply defines the area of revelation. Action and decision-making do not necessarily mean that the person launches forth in war or in a special program of social reform, but it does mean that he "speaks for" God. Speaking—saying the word of God—is an expression of truth through personality, and it is an expression of commitment as well as a word of comfort, guidance, or exhortation. The Bible was originally almost entirely a spoken word to the people of God about the meaning of faith in the affairs of the world in which they lived.

A fourth characteristic of revelation as an experience is inner certainty. A person who in the midst of the human situation about him knows what God would have him say in relationship to that situation, has an experience which gives him an inner authority. He knows what he must do regardless of its effect on him or the opinions others will hold about him or the misunderstanding he may create among his friends. This certainty is not achieved by logical inquiry or by hunch or intuition. It comes from God and is related to the human situation in which the person lives. A person is conscious that he knows the will of God even though he cannot explain the experience or prove by any rational means the basis of his experience; he may not even understand why this experience should have happened to him.

We must not give the impression that this type of experience is restricted to great leaders in the Bible, such as Moses or Isaiah. The same experience in a less spectacular way takes place regularly. It is not unusual for a young person in college to come to a realization that there is a divine constraint operating in his life, leading him to a vocation through which he can serve the Kingdom of God. Often he is bewildered by the unexpected turn of events and is at a loss to explain the change which is taking place in his own life. Yet, with increasing confidence he turns his whole life in a different direction. From the depth of his being he finds a new serenity of spirit and confidence for his future in the midst of all the previous plans that have been broken by his new understanding of himself and his relation to God. Revelation causes a person to see himself, his world, and his future differently, and this new orientation is pivoted on an authority that takes charge of his inner being. The person is not suddenly different, for all his old habits, temptations, skills, and abilities are still with him; but he can now see them differently and can energize them around new goals. The world in which he lives is the same, but he sees it differently and perceives more clearly what he must do to be God's agent of redemption. When revelation occurs, a person is conscious of an inner authority that "makes all things new" (Revelation 21:1-5).

LEARNING THROUGH EVENTS

We started with tradition and saw the person first experiencing life according to the structure of meaning which characterizes the adults who nurtured him. Revelation is likewise an experience, but it breaks through the culture and gives the receiver a meaningful word about himself and the human situation for which he must take responsibility.

But whether a person is learning life or learning to know God or, as is usually the case, doing both simultaneously, he does so through events. Events are difficult to describe even though they are the substance that makes up our lives. Perhaps this is because the closer we get to reality, the more intensely personal the experience becomes and therefore the less easy it is to describe in an objective way. The more an experience means to us, the more difficulty we have in describing it and the more emotionally charged is our account. Our being is so involved that we not only interpret the event from the point of our presupposition, but we also vigorously defend what we say and do, because our own selfhood is at stake. Moreover, we often find that we have to say the same thing over two or three different times to try to convey our meaning to another person. In contrast, when we describe an experience that is not important to us, we can do so rather easily in a calm, objective way.

The Bible gives us an account of events through which God made his will known. We do not have abstract data about God; we have accounts of God's guidance in relation to specific happenings. Theologians have studied these accounts and have worked out descriptions of God, such as the Shorter Catechism definition that "God is a Spirit, infinite, eternal, and unchangeable, in his being, wisdom, power, holiness, justice, goodness, and truth."[15] Although this definition is Biblical, it is not found in that form in the Bible. Rather, we have one event in the Bible that shows God as just, another event that shows him as good, etc.; and these have been put in logical order by theologians. It is necessary to co-ordinate what we know about God from separate events into a system in order to understand our faith. But faith itself is not dependent on a person's having a co-ordinated, integrated mental scheme about God. Theology is a mental process that is significant only after a person has some knowledge of, and faith in, God. Prior to formalized, intellectual statements about God are experiences with God, either those which are uniquely one's own, or participation in the experiences that have been recorded in the Bible. In either case, learning to know God and his will comes through human events.

An understanding of events is important because events are the context in which learning takes place and they supply the reality from which the learning is derived. We should at this point be clear about what we mean by learning. Learning is not the "other side" of teaching. Teaching is a deliberate, organized effort to transmit information, skills, attitudes, or belief; and in this sense teaching constitutes the bulk of our educational effort in the church. But learning is what a person actually appropriates from the reality to which he responds. Learning comes from events, and what is learned is tested in subsequent events.

I do not want to depreciate the role of knowledge, information, or the natural reasoning power of the mind in understanding the Christian faith; but these elements will not in themselves, nor in any combination, produce faith in God. Yet these elements are indispensable in faith because the mind must be used to struggle with events. Knowledge of the Bible, doctrine, and history are essential in order to know and properly understand the present situation. Perhaps we will have to say simply, "By grace are ye saved through faith; and that not of yourselves: it is the gift of God" (Ephesians 2:8, k.j.v.). To the extent that Christian faith can be learned, it is learned through events. Therefore, we must attempt to understand the nature of events in order to see how they can be utilized for the practical work of the church.

Events are units of meaning. An event is not a person or a set of circumstances. It is a particular combination of both that can be described and, with some degree of faithfulness, re-enacted. We can seldom tell what a person's motive is by looking at his actions, and we can never understand the precise way a person evaluates all the factors that enter his mind in making a decision. But we can observe what he does and says in relation to facts and forces that face him. Indeed, the significant part of a person is known only in his relation to the events which make up his life. The circumstances of an event can be recorded so that later these circumstances can be re-created in the mind, then the human emotions that engulfed the facts can be supplied by the imagination. With this imaginary reconstruction of a human event in mind, we can then see the significance of the human actors who took it upon themselves in the name of God to change the conditions they experienced. More facts about Jesus (his height, weight, etc.) give us no important help in understanding our Lord. We know Jesus primarily in relationship to first-century Judaism in Palestine, a segment of the Roman Empire. We know him better when we see him contending with temptations (Matthew 4:1-11), discussing eternal life with a rich young ruler (Mark 10:17-31) or a lawyer (Luke 10:25-37), healing on the Sabbath in the presence of Pharisees (Luke 14:1-6), commenting on a poor widow as she puts pennies in the offering (Luke 21:1-4), demonstrating true greatness by washing the disciples' feet (John 13:3-5; Luke 22:24-27), and above all in his arrest, trial, betrayal, crucifixion, and resurrection. Even the bulk of his teachings has come to us in parables, which are events created by imagination.

Events are educational by their very nature. The circumstances of an event elicit our response. Circumstances of an event draw us into thought, word, or action so that we feel we must respond to the conditions we face. One of the peculiar things about an event is that we are drawn into action even if our participation in the event is not successful or even if we know in advance that our efforts will not be successful. The very nature of an event causes us to participate in order to live up to our true self, to the values about which we have built our life. This intense and deep self-participation requires that our whole being be alert to the conditions that we are meeting. For example, it might be a very simple thing such as working and voting for a particular political candidate; in the end the election might be lost, but we would perhaps feel gratified that the issues were made clear and that we had worked to improve the community in which we lived. Our involvement in an event and our concern for the outcome of an event are factors which define the circle of things that make up an event, and they are the factors that make an event a powerful learning experience.

The learning that takes place in events is never neutral. It is never information that may or may not be used or an experience that can be easily forgotten. Eventful learning is always colored by emotion which was generated in the experience. We all know that a teacher may teach mathematics and we may learn enough to pass an examination; but we may also learn to hate math and may never voluntarily take more courses in that subject. Or, to use the illustration of the political campaign again, we may learn in the political campaign that politics can be fun and creative at the same time, even though our candidate loses!

Eventful learning is specific. We learn certain things in certain situations. This does not mean that we can also learn to transpose that learning to another situation. For example, a child learns to be honest in making change because his parents insist on it and the storekeepers expect it; but he learns to lie about his age in order to get a children's ticket to the theatre because his parents require it and the gatekeeper does not question the deception. A child usually has a crazy-quilt conception of honesty. He hears his parents lie on the telephone about engagements and then insist that he tell the truth about where he has been after school. Out of all the variety of experiences he has with honesty, he does not so much develop the generalized trait of honesty as he develops a knowledge of honesty in a series of situations, in some of which he may be dishonest without hurting his moral code. One of his biggest problems is in trying to find out which is which—in relating the specific experiences of honesty to the general idea of honesty.

Events are social. They involve the interaction of people within a commonly perceived situation. Perhaps it would be helpful to use the word "situation" to connote the describable facts, conditions, attitudes, opportunities, goals, and other factors that people face and to which they must react. It would be analogous to the plot and setting of a play. The persons involved in an event are like actors. We can see their physical characteristics, hear their verbal understanding of themselves, and surmise the emotional impulses which motivate them; but "the play's the thing," as Hamlet said, "wherein I'll catch the conscience of the king" (Act II, Scene II, line 641). So an event is made up of persons and situations, but the event is the over-all "thing" that actually happens. The close relationship of play and event is normal, for a play is an imaginary event. Or turned the other way around, it can be said that the Biblical events are best told in story and drama—just as the Bible does—because in these literary forms we are as close as possible to real events; and real events, as in a play, involve a group of people in mutual interaction. In human events a move or word from one person prompts a move or word from a second person, while the first person modifies or changes his position in the light of the second person's move, and so it goes. We all attempt to plan events or at least to control our participation in events. However, events seldom work out as planned. Life involves so many people and so many circumstances of illness, accident, and personal whim that no preconceived scheme is adequate for all contingencies. Therefore, we continually modify our desires in relationship to the other people who are involved in the events of our life.

Events may be defined as the "given" of life—such as the age, sex, race, language, physical limitations, or economic circumstances of the people involved. Other elements in an event are not predetermined, such as illness, accident, death of a political leader, revolution, economic depression. Although these elements are given in the structure of a society in which one lives and in the particular configuration of facts which faces a person, the person has a "say," sometimes a decisive "say," as to how much of the given of life he will allow to coagulate into events. An extreme example is the autistic child who refuses to communicate with people. A common illustration is the person who restricts his world to family, job, and recreation and refuses to interact with, or assume responsibility for, anything else; he has no interest in seeking a deeper satisfaction in the events in which he is engaged. Even though a person can limit the given of life to which he will respond, this does not mean that he can control the events in which he is engaged. A person can radically cut down the scope of reality to which he will respond in order to be somewhat adequate as a person to the reality to which he must respond. Stated this way, we see that an important function of Christian education is to increase a person's awareness of the world to which he may respond and to help him become more sensitive to the leading of God's Spirit in the situations in which he must act. Increasing awareness may be developed in the realm of ideas, in the depth of oneself, in the range of human problems that can be comprehended, or in understanding the interrelatedness of these matters. Christian education might also help a person to expect and to see in his ever-widening awareness the will of God for these events.

Events are bits of reality. We have already defined reality as that to which a person responds, but reality imposes itself on us in small pieces. Life is like a moving picture. The film in a movie is a series of still pictures which, when shown in succession, give the impression of motion. Events are something like that. They are specific. They occur in a definite time and place even if they continue for weeks or months. They are unique. Events happen a certain way and will not be repeated that same way again. Events are rather well-defined although one event may impinge on another or blend into another. However, the event has a unity to it which makes it separate enough to report, analyze, and remember. Stringing events together gives us the sense of movement in our life; and some events, like some scenes in a movie, are decisive ones for many of the smaller or ordinary events that follow.

Because events are bits of reality, they usually involve conflict.

At this point they form a close association with drama. A play would be scarcely worth seeing (indeed, would it be a play at all?) if it did not have conflict between characters, within a person, or between causes to which one might give himself. To see unrelated actions, words, or living conditions on the stage would have no significance. An event has a multitude of parts, but they are related; they are also in conflict, because each human being involved is trying to shape the parts to fit his convenience or his will. If he were not so energized, he would not be dealing with what he thinks is real. Matters on which we readily compromise or about which we argue little are matters that do not fundamentally affect our understanding of reality. We can probably say that the closer we get to reality, the sharper will be our conflicts. Specifically, this means that if we expect our educational work in the church to be related to the actual problems people face, we have to be prepared to face conflict. This in turn means we will have to have the emotional strength to handle the conflict and the skill to turn the discussion into paths which will develop self-understanding in relationship to real problems, rather than letting the conflict itself become the problem. Kindergarten teachers expect conflict, even physical blows; they handle it not by saying, "Tut, tut, let's stop fighting," but by trying to find a reason why the fight was started, thus helping the fighters develop self-understanding in relation to the struggle. If we could do a similar thing with adults, we would be able to open up, as the subject matter of Christian education, the whole range of problems that adults face, and not confine our efforts to areas in which there is already general agreement.

SUMMARY

We have been saying that reality is that which we face, to which we are constrained to react. We experience reality in events, a unit of meaning which combines persons and circumstances. Learning takes place according to a person's participation in events and is conditioned by his awareness of what is happening, by his personal characteristics and abilities, and by the perceptual system that has been built into him by his culture. Revelation comes through human events. God is known in things that happen rather than in speculative reason, and the Biblical record is primarily a description of events and the meaning of these events for the believing community.

Today the agents of faith communication—parents, adults, small groups in the church—have to see that tradition and experience are bound up in events. On the one hand, we use events to show what our belief-system means in relation to what happens. On the other hand, we have to be sensitive to events in order to get a fresh understanding of God's activity in the world. Both the conservation and the creative adaptation of tradition are bound up in the dynamic process of passing it on. Therefore, we must be much clearer about the way in which we use events that are happening—and events we cause to happen—as the key to our communication of faith.

IV

Faith and Self-Identification

Let us review our case thus far. Culture is the reality with which we must deal. And culture—insofar as it presents a way of life and therefore functions as a religion—is communicated through a process of socialization which (1) establishes a perceptive system in relation to a world view, (2) forms a conscience according to a value system, and (3) creates a self-identification out of personal relations within a social group. Religion in our Western world is a subculture that communicates itself in the same way, religion and culture being mixed in a variety of ways according to the specific religious tradition. The Christian faith is likewise a mixture. It presents special problems because we believe that although revelation from God in the past has a claim upon us in the present, we have to be open to experience with God in the present which may modify our past understanding of God. Events are the units of life in which past revelation and present experience are united; therefore they are the building blocks out of which we erect our life of faith.

The three processes have content, but this content is not abstract knowledge or information that can be easily abandoned or manipulated in the mind. The content is personal knowledge. It is the type attributed to Paul when he says, "But I am not ashamed, for I know whom I have believed, and I am sure that he is able to guard until that Day what has been entrusted to me" (2 Timothy 1:12). It is a sentiment ("thought or judgment permeated with feeling") that relates to the whole person.

The three processes go on incessantly as adults in their roles as parents, friends, relatives, government officials, teachers, train children. But adults do not stand by themselves as autonomous individuals; they are molded and maintained as persons by the groups to which they belong. It is in the kinship, work, play, neighborhood, club, or church groups which they select and to which they give themselves that adults have self-identification. Adult group life is the source of the content of the socialization process and is the means by which adults are trained to be socializers.

Applying this socialization process to the communication of the Christian faith requires that we start with the group of adult believers. The natural communication process starts with, and is nourished by, the community of believers. It is in such community that adults find themselves, obtain emotional security, reinforce and reinterpret the Christian world view and value system, find strength to resist other interpretations of life, and are coached on how to play their role as communicators of faith. The community of believers is the home of the Christian. An individual could not be Christian without constant fellowship with "kindred minds." Christian self-identification is the result of participation in the church.

IMAGES OF THE CHURCH

Generally, we have been avoiding the word "church" in order not to equate our present denominational pattern or our large, successful, clublike congregations with the New Testament ideas of the church. These modern manifestations of the church may be, or may become, the real church; but it is more important for our purpose to focus our attention on what a group of believers should be and do if it would take seriously its responsibility to communicate faith in the God of the Bible.

When we turn to the New Testament to get our clues, we find that many conceptions were used by the church in self-explanation, but no one of these ideas displaced the others. Paul Minear in his study of the analogies used for the church by New Testament writers counts a total of 96. Most of these are minor images such as God's field (1 Corinthians 3:9), a building on a rock (Matthew

16:18), bride of Christ (2 Corinthians 11:1-2), or the Dispersion (James 1:1 and 1 Peter 1:1). The major images are the people of God (1 Peter 2:9-10; Romans 9:25-26), the new creation (2 Corinthians 5:17), the fellowship in faith (1 Corinthians 1:2; Acts 26:18), and the body of Christ (Romans 12:4-5; 1 Corinthians 12:12-31).[1]

These images of the church were in tension with the empirical manifestation of the church. They represented the "oughtness" of the church—the way the church defined and explained herself to herself and to the world. We should not call these images the invisible church; such a designation is misleading because it suggests an order of reality beyond the world, seriously diverts attention from the church as it is, and implies that there is something other than the empirical church in which God is interested. Rather, we should accept the images of the church for what they are—mental constructs of crucial importance in clarifying the church's self-understanding and in relating the memory of God's past activity to contemporary circumstances.

But the New Testament also describes the empirical church. Within the community of believers there were divisions (1 Corinthians 1:11-17); there was dishonesty (Acts 5:1-6); false teachers emerged (2 Corinthians 11:13); insincere members defected (2 Timothy 4:10); and class distinctions imperiled the equality of believers (James 2:1-5). From New Testament times until today we have had these problems within the church.

COMMUNAL REALITY

In spite of all of the sins, inconsistencies, and human failures reported in the New Testament church, the church grew, stabilized itself, created a literature that has been normative for the Christian faith, developed a government, trained leaders, hammered out ethical principles for the day-to-day problems, and within a few hundred years spread throughout the Roman Empire. The literary remains of this powerful and creative expansion of faith show that the church was a fellowship of people who believed that in Jesus of Nazareth God had visited and redeemed his people. Christ did not rely on a book or creed to spread the faith but trained a group of men who, after the resurrection, embodied his life and teachings. As Christ was the incarnation of God, so the community of believers continued the presence of Christ; it existed to worship, to serve its members, and to minister to the world in the name of Jesus (Acts 2:38-42; 4:5-12; 4:30; 5:27-32; 9:27, etc.).

There are many terms in the New Testament that are translated into the English word "church," but the principal term, *ecclesia,* is a rather neutral term. Minear points out that *"Ecclesia* was used primarily to designate a particular communal reality, not to describe its qualitative aspects."[2] The New Testament writers used almost one hundred figures of speech in an attempt to get substantive meaning into the word "church." But we must note that *ecclesia* designates the particular communal reality that underlies both the images of the church and the empirical church. "In more than seventy-five passages, scattered through at least fifteen New Testament books, there are abundant data to support the thought of the church as the community of believers."[3] (For example, see Matthew 18:15-20; John 17:20-21; Acts 2:44-47; 4:32-35; 1 Corinthians 12; Ephesians 1:1; Colossians 1:2; Hebrews 4:3, 9.) Claude Welch has come to the conclusion that "There is no purely private Christianity, for to be in Christ is to be in the church, and to be in the church is to be in Christ, and any attempt to separate relation to Christ in faith from membership in the church is a perversion of the New Testament understanding."[4]

Where do we find this communal reality that is the substructure of the church? Perhaps the best general answer comes from Matthew's Gospel, where the disciples are reported to be in a dialogue with Jesus about the church; here the church is defined in these words, "Where two or three are gathered in my name, there am I in the midst of them" (Matthew 18:20). This communal reality is found in a self-conscious association of believers who are permanent enough in location to have face-to-face relationships with each other in a variety of situations and who are stable enough to function as a corporate group in carrying out their mutually developed plans and activities. Normally, this would be the local congregation; yet we do not want to limit the church to the local congregation. Some congregations are so large and so organized and administered that interaction between persons in a meaningful manner is virtually impossible. Also, the communal reality can develop in structures apart from the local congregation. New forms of Christian association may develop, modeled along lines other than the congregation. But for practical purposes and under normal circumstances, I would say that the communal reality is most readily experienced in the local congregation. Or, put it the other way around: the local congregation should be of such size and so organized that the communal reality can most readily develop and be experienced by its members.

Today there is a small, well-informed, articulate group of Christian leaders who seriously doubt that the congregation can be the church. Critics of the congregational structure of the church say that the congregation is based on residence and is an illustration of the old adage that birds of a feather flock together. The congregation tends to consist of people of the same race, class, and interests. Moreover, the congregation under these circumstances will often follow the motif of pietism which Gibson Winter identifies as a preoccupation with private values such as the home, the nurture of children, the maintenance of moral virtues, and personal mental health.[5] Such a congregation, according to Winter, will seldom develop the motif of servanthood in which the congregation sees its task as preparing its members to work within the structures of society in order to minister to the community. Winter has proposed to free "the suburban captivity of the church" by a "sector" plan whereby the residential slice of the congregation will be pie-shaped, with the wide part of the pie in the suburbs and the pointed end in the inner city. This sector-residential base would necessitate a mixture of races and classes and force attention of the congregation on the pressing urban problems and worldly concerns of their common life. A congregation with a residential base that includes all sorts and conditions of men, it is thought, would not be an easy retreat from political responsibility, vocational responsibility, or social justice.

Another source of criticism comes from various study commissions of the World Council of Churches and is summarized in a recent book, *Where in the World?*[6] Here the residential base of the local congregation is more severely and systematically attacked, probably because these reports are dominated by European leaders living in countries with a state church and a geographically formed parish system. Nevertheless, one receives the impression from reading these reports that the congregation as such has outlived its usefulness and that we should enter a new era where the church must "let the world write the agenda" and then allow its ministry to "take shape around the needs of the world."[7]

There is much about this fresh way of stating the role of the church in facing the problems of the world that we should encourage. The church everywhere—not just in Europe—has too often looked after its own concerns, has dealt with the state only at those points where the state could strengthen the church as an institution, and has related itself to worldly concerns only through a few unusual laymen who attempted to find new ways to solve human problems. Current discussion about the necessity of the church's being a servant and about helping the laity to work as Christians in the ordinary problems of life reminds us that the church has a task to continue the ministry of Christ in the world—that the church is not an end in itself. Such an emphasis will help us play down building programs and concentrate more on what we should be doing as Christians. The servant church will remind us that Christ is Lord of the church and that we are to seek his mind for the church's work. But when all of this is said, have we really eliminated the local congregation? Or have we not said that the congregation as it now exists in many places is not effectively living up to its task?

THE GATHERED CHRISTIANS

Although other forms of the church exist, the basic unit remains the congregation. The congregation itself may, because of its residential nature, have difficulty being the church; but such problems could be solved by something like Gibson Winter's sector church or by a congregation's deliberate effort to overcome the class or racial bias that exists in the community in which it is located. The important factor is not residence but *the basis on which the congregation is formed*. If the congregation is formed on the basis of belief in Jesus Christ as God's revelation to men and if the believers give their allegiance to Christ, then the residential basis of the believing community is not a detracting factor. The lordship of Christ, *if taken seriously,* will lead the congregation into a constant evaluation of all forms of life, personal and social.

Many of the new forms of mission—the effort to be in the world at points of need such as in coffee houses and on ski slopes, in national parks, with drug addicts, with laborers in factories, with vocational groups such as business and professional men, with artists and entertainers—are the finest sort of evangelism; but the question still remains, "What happens next?" If we communicate with groupings of people about the vocational basis of their life and attempt to translate the Christian faith into the language and thought forms of these groupings, when an individual responds do we leave him alone, do we continue our ministry to him on an individual basis, or do we gather such people together on a regular basis and form a believing community? All of these strategies are possible, but it is my contention that until believers are gathered together in a conscious, voluntary fellowship with a common allegiance to Christ, they are not the church.

Why this insistence on the communal nature of the church? Because it is by this process that faith can be incubated and nurtured. Faith is a concomitant of human association. That is why the church must be a gathering of Christians which is permanent enough to allow individuals to know each other in various facets of their life and regular enough in its meetings to be able to develop a sense of solidarity in Christ and in their mission to the world. The human interaction is the most powerful process we know for creating and sustaining values, affections, commitments; for shaping a distinctive style of life; and for commanding loyalty greater than life itself. "Greater love has no man than this," said Jesus, "that a man lay down his life for his friends" (John 15:13).

The interactional process is not in itself faith, nor does it have any particular ideology of its own. The process is human and works in secular gatherings as well as in the church. The process communicates whatever is lived; and the extent to which the gathered Christians have faith and are searching for the will of God is the extent to which they will be able to communicate those elements in their lives to each other, to their children, and to the world where they work and play.

Kirk Lewin, one of our keenest students of human nature, said that learning is first a new belonging. By this he meant that a person is not open to change until in his deepest being he feels that he belongs to a group. Then he incorporates voluntarily and eagerly what the group represents and what he learns in the group. It is in this sense that the church by its communal nature is an educational enterprise. The self-conscious human group worshiping, living, and working together is a learning community. To dissect the living community into parts is to give the impression that the whole is just the sum of the parts. But if we will keep in mind that the parts do have special functions which contribute to the whole, we may explore in more detail how each of the following four functions contributes to the communal reality that underlies the church.

Worship Incubates Faith

First, the congregation through worship incubates faith. Worship is a corporate act of adoration, praise, and thankfulness which has characterized the Christian church from its beginning. Regardless of how widespread the activities of a congregation may be, worship is the central act. Regardless of how diligently the church may be persecuted and threatened by hostile rulers, worship rallies the faithful, nourishes their souls, and remains the irreducible minimum of their life together. We cannot explore this area in detail, but we must identify its central importance for the communication of faith and note the way in which worship is related to personal religious experience.

We do not have empirical studies to prove that corporate worship is a decisive factor in the communication of faith; however, our religious common sense and the personal experiences of many Christians would so testify. The gathering of believers to express their belief through prayer, song, reading and explanation of Scripture, to confess their sin, and to celebrate the sacraments is the very essence of the Christian faith. In these acts of worship we express our commitment to God. Such acts can be a combination of our deepest yearning, our strongest emotions, our finest thoughts. The fact that worship combines these elements of our life is what gives worship the power to communicate. To see a person you know kneel in prayer is to have his testimony that God is, that God is available for guidance and strength, and that the believer recognizes the contingencies and limitations of his life in the total scheme of things. Worship springs from levels of our being deeper than our reason. It is motivated by sentiment more powerful than our will. That is why worship communicates; it is the whole person demonstrating what faith is.

We must also note the way worship is related to personal experience. Christian worship is not personal in the sense of being an experience that centers on the person. That is why too much attention to mood music, lights, temperature, and decoration is a basic misunderstanding of worship. That is why the experience of beauty in nature or art—although it may produce the feeling of awe, wonder, and excitement—is not distinctively Christian worship. An aesthetic experience can be enjoyed by a person with many kinds of religious belief or a person of no religious persuasion. Not even the psychological experience of "insight" wherein we suddenly see new depths of meaning in ourself is in itself the goal of worship.

What is unique in Christian worship is an experience with the God of the Bible. It is experience of the most intense kind and is personal to the extent that one feels that the whole world is less real than the presence of God; but the difference is that one experiences the God who is described in the Bible. That is why it is so important to read the Psalms—to catch the flavor of their devotion, to relive the affirmations they made about God—or to sing the songs of the Christian church throughout the centuries and thereby renew our relation with the past. Likewise, we read and expound the Scriptures because we have in the past revelation of God an image of God that can be activated in our mind by the Holy Spirit. So, to discuss worship only in terms of experience is not enough. Christian worship is an activity in which a person participates in order to relive the traditions of the faith and to explore the images of God displayed in the Bible.

The true meaning of worship is seen in the celebration of the sacraments. In both sacraments we do something within the local congregation of believers which is completely dependent on the past action of God. In baptism we renew for a child the covenant in Christ, and the congregation pledges to help raise the child in the "nurture and admonition" of the Lord. In the Lord's Supper we have an even more powerful re-enactment of the gospel. The body of believers gathers to partake of the body and blood of Christ, so there is symbolic incorporation of Christ into one's life and a profound reminder of what God has done for us in Christ's death and resurrection. Moreover, the corporate nature of the sacrament reminds us of our dependence on each other if we are to be an authentic part of Christ's body and share in his ministry to the world.

Likewise, preaching should be an effort to appropriate the past for the present. If we do not take our image of God from the Bible, we substitute our own religious experience for an authentic knowledge of God. We might put it more strongly by saying that unless we go back to the Biblical revelation to find our guidelines, we will not be able to transcend the cultural situation in which we live and therefore will not be able to understand the present.

Such a statement will jar segments of American Protestantism because we still have a residue of nineteenth-century revivalism and early twentieth-century liberalism in our midst. These two movements were antithetical in most respects, representing two different types of theology. They were alike in their insistence on personal religious experience. In revivalism this was a personal conversion experience. In liberalism it was individual insight into the nature of things, especially the gradual evolutionary development of man and his maturing sense of social responsibility. In neither movement was the Biblical revelation in its full historical sweep taken seriously. This is seen particularly in the revivalist's lack of concern for social justice and the liberal's disregard for the way sin has permeated every part of our being, disrupting all plans for improving the social and political order.

If we turn to the Bible, we do not find personal experience made normative. Let us look at the Apostle Paul, for example, because his conversion experience has been used as a standard pattern of religious experience. Actually, Paul seldom refers to his religious experience and he does not make his experience the basis of Christian theology. When he does refer to his personal religious experience, he does so reluctantly.[8] In fact, Paul plays down his own religious experience "so that no one may think more of me than he sees in me or hears from me" (2 Corinthians 12; see especially verse 6). Rather, Paul's sermons are mainly a review of the history of Israel used to interpret Christ, or his sermons relate particular events in the lives of his auditors to the revelation of God that is recorded in their Scripture. When Paul used his conversion experience in his sermon before the Jewish people in Jerusalem, he used his experience not as a basis for the Christian's life, but to show how he came to know Jesus of Nazareth as the Christ (Acts 22:1-21). In his defense before Agrippa, Paul compressed his experience even more and spent much of his time showing how he was not "disobedient to the heavenly vision" as he went through the country telling people they should "repent and turn to God and perform deeds worthy of their repentance" and "saying nothing but what the prophets and Moses said would come to pass . . ." (Acts 26:19-23). Paul's preaching method is clear: a person must have religious experience but it should be experience with God who is known from the scriptural record.

Guidance is also found in the way Paul had to handle other people's religious experience within the church. There was a strong movement in the Corinthian church to give special attention to people who spoke in tongues, thus making experience the basis of the Christian faith. Paul's discussion of this problem is a fine example of the role of experience in the Christian life (1 Corinthians 14). Paul does not want to diminish the mystery that surrounds the revelation from God, nor does he want to assume that nothing new can come from God. He recognizes that a person's experience with God must be respected and honored, but there is an important test that must be used for such experience—the words must make sense in relation to what we already know about God. Thus, a person who has a religious experience must "pray for the power to interpret" (verse 13). The test is *the ability to instruct others in the church,* and that is why Paul said he "would rather speak five words with my mind, in order to instruct others, than ten thousand words in a tongue" (verse 19). Paul continued his discussion of worship by saying that when they came together, the hymn, Scripture reading, and interpretation should be selected and used for "edification" (verse 26). Paul considered worship an experience of faith through understanding the past revelation of God rather than a person's private experience. The purpose of worship is to enable us to understand and glorify God, not to enter into an aesthetic, insightful, or ecstatic emotional state, although all of these may be used to bring one closer to God.

These comments about worship are brief because worship is one facet of the congregational life that has maintained the distinctive marks of the gospel more than the other functions we shall discuss. Regardless of how poor the quality, worship has consistently been a corporate matter as believers gathered together around their common obligation to Christ. The preaching, insofar as it has followed Scripture, has helped the congregation see beyond the confines of culture. The celebration of the sacraments has regularly brought the past revelation of God into the believer's present and in an environment of faith has offered the believers a physical connection with the revelation of God in Jesus Christ. Regardless of age, a person has the seeds of faith planted in his being by a worshiping congregation. These seeds are watered and nurtured by a person's own prayers and Bible reading and by participation in a family which incorporates the Christian virtues.

Fellowship Makes Faith Operational

Second, the fellowship of believers makes faith operational. Faith is an experience which can be thought about but cannot be produced by thinking. It is like hope and love in that it comes into our being through our associations and is strengthened through experience in our daily living. Put in practical terms, a person learns the meaning of love and how to love as a baby through his relation to his parents. If this relationship is distorted or if love is absent, the baby is emotionally deformed and will grow into a twisted person. There is no way to tell a baby about love—it is something that has to be inculcated through the actions of the adults who surround the child. So these greatest of Christian words, faith, hope, and love, do not express ideas about, but are symbols of, human qualities that are found in, and communicated by, a believing community. Let us look more closely at the role of the believing community in making faith operational.

Words must be related to experience. Words are symbols. We learn word symbols in relationship to objects, so that teaching a child to talk is a natural and relatively easy type of teaching. We identify a word with the proper object whenever the child is ready. This teaching is done normally in the home and is done so casually that we do not recognize the profundity of the process. Probably no learning is more fundamental to all later development than the ability to talk. We forget too quickly how we coached the child and rewarded him with love and attention when he pronounced a word properly and related it to the correct object.

The believing community through its own life and indirectly through the parents is constantly teaching words such as faith, hope, and love to the children in the church. Through sermons, stories, teaching conversation, and songs, this community relates words to descriptions of what the words mean. The individual is trained by the congregation to identify these words and their meaning. The most powerful form of this training is the lived experience. Let's take forgiveness as an example. Its centrality in the Christian faith is unquestioned. "Forgive us our debts, as we forgive our debtors" is one of the most important petitions in the Lord's Prayer and is the only one that Jesus singled out for special attention (Matthew 6:12, K.J.V.; 6:14-15). Forgiveness looms large in the teachings of Jesus, and the theology of the cross is built on the affirmation that God, through Christ's sacrifice, forgives. But these affirmations about forgiveness have to be understood within experience. The parable of the Unforgiving Servant and other teachings of our Lord all show that forgiveness has to be "situationalized"; that is, it must be made a part of one's experience or it has no value (Matthew 18:21-35). Paul shows exactly how this must be done in the Corinthian church when he requests the church to forgive and comfort a member who has caused pain to Paul and the congregation (2 Corinthians 2:5-10).

The only way forgiveness can be learned today is for a person to be forgiven, and this requires a community where forgiveness is expected and practiced. The community is necessary because the specific things for which one needs forgiveness happen in relation to other people in a continuous stream of human interaction; and the forgiveness has to be given, in part, by the persons who have been pained. Mail-order forgiveness—or any kind of forgiveness that does not allow for remorse and restitution among the people where the act took place or among those who care about the outcome—is impossible.

Experience must be related to the affirmations of faith. There is a sense in which faith, hope, and love are common human experiences and therefore exist apart from the Christian congregation. Here we are faced with two alternatives. We can say on the one hand that the Christian religion overlaps cultural values at these points. Such an approach emphasizes the nature of the human experience rather than its source and maintains that love is love wherever found—indeed, that love is God. Such an approach puts a premium on the human; it can never be satisfactory to the Christian because it cuts the nerve of faith. To say love is God is to deify human experience. On the other hand, we can say God is love, and this love is a particular kind of sacrificial love that initiates and maintains a relationship in spite of the other person's arrogant misuse of love. For the Christian, the words faith, hope, and love have a reference—God. The reference gives a special quality to the words. The Christian does not put his faith in life but in God. He does not love because he wants others to love him but because God first loved him; he does not hope in the gradual development of the race or in human goodness but in God's providence and God's guidance.

It is the relating of these experiences to God that makes the community of believers necessary. This is true not only because faith is described in the Bible as always related to Israel or the church but also because the community, rather than the individual, is the depository of the belief system. The community of believers transcends the individual and therefore is able to maintain the belief that God is the reference for faith even when the individual loses his faith or passes from the community.

Faith-affirmations must be kept in balance. As long as faith-affirmations stand close to the experience they describe, the affirmation has a built-in understanding. The parable of the Prodigal Sons tells such a common story that we can readily understand forgiveness if it means an action or an attitude such as the father's (Luke 15:11-32). However, when faith-affirmations become abstract—more a symbol in the mind than an identification of experience—then there is danger that the belief statements will be out of balance. One of the classic unsolved problems in the church is the relationship between the doctrines of law and of grace. A library of books has been written on these subjects and their interrelationship, but the prior question is, "Can one solve a problem in human relations by logical mental processes?" The answer is no. Although logic is helpful in clarifying and relating ideas, human problems cannot be solved this way. Human problems, in the final analysis, have to be adjudicated.

The basic issue is not new. When Gentiles in Rome (untouched by the moral wisdom of the Jews) became Christians, they heard with pleasure that God was good in spite of evil and that God forgave in spite of sin. When this was put in their minds as a proposition, some people thought they could now do evil and good would come or that they were free to sin in order to enjoy forgiveness. To both of these propositions Paul reacted sharply (Romans 6:1-19), not only because the people were wrong in their assumption about God but also because such an analysis assumed faith to be a private matter unrelated to the total needs of the believing community. Faith and the outworking of faith is a corporate experience. One has to act for the welfare of the group, and therefore one cannot do evil or sin deliberately without damage to the Body of Christ. When one realizes that his faith is directly related to the welfare of the believing community, he is forced to test his intellectual formulations of faith by the way they affect the group (Romans 14:1—15:13).

There is another sense in which the body of believers is essential for achieving a balance in doctrine. Doctrinal statements must be translated into action. In other places, I have indicated the impossibility of taking a general principle and applying it uniformly to life situations. There is always something about the life situation which has an integrity of its own that conditions to some extent the general doctrinal proposition. Many people, for example, extract from the life of our Lord his statements about God's love, quoting John 3:16, and then generalize that love is the only significant facet to our relationship with God. Such people forget Jesus' cleansing the Temple with the whip in his hand or the dreadful woes against the Pharisees quoted in Matthew 23. Likewise, we center on Paul's incomparable hymn of love in 1 Corinthians 13 without balancing it with his strict moral judgments in the same letter (see 1 Corinthians 5:1-2). The church at Corinth had to reconcile both love and moral law and we have to do it in the same way, through a believing community.

The congregation is not the sum of individual believers. It is a dynamic, living reality that adjusts, adapts, modifies, and makes exception to general faith propositions which come from the past. In this sense the congregation is a method of communication when it relates human conditions to faith-affirmations, making whatever interpretation is necessary for the conditions that obtain locally.

Searching Makes Faith Meaningful

Third, the community of believers through its searching of the Scriptures makes faith meaningful.[9] I have avoided the word "study" because that word too often means an examination of materials without clear-cut purpose, without a determination to find meaning in relation to life. Searching connotes the use of many resources to arrive at a goal, and this better describes the need for enlisting all mental faculties in our effort to understand faith.

Biblical faith is not a vague, foglike aspiration to do good nor a generalized holiness of life nor even a force that underlies the beings of the world. Biblical faith is welded to the image of God that is etched in Biblical history. We believe the apostolic interpretation stands as our norm of "faith and practice." But this apostolic norm has to be presented to and accepted by individuals, and this is an indispensable function of the congregation. Since the congregation will interpret that norm in its presentation, the congregation must be aware of what it is doing and what it means as it communicates the Christian tradition.

The effort to describe and communicate the faith was the purpose that produced most of the Biblical material. This process, which we can see at work in the book of Acts, probably lies behind most of the New Testament books. The process is an interactional procedure whereby out of argument, discussion, preaching and discussion of preaching, instruction and discussion of instruction, and normal human conversation which flows back and forth over topics of common interest, a mentality is developed which in turn forms and informs the believers. If we start with Acts 13:16, we will read Paul's sermon in Antioch and note that at the end of the sermon people begged him to continue at the synagogue on the next Saturday. Surely Paul, Barnabas, and the converts did not become silent between Sabbaths. They must have had a lively week of conversation and argument, because the next appearance touched off a riot. The well-known fifteenth chapter fascinates us. We see here the clash between Paul and Barnabas on the one hand and the Judaizers on the other, but we should not overlook the method that was used. After the clash of opinion, there was "much debate" (verse 7) and a giving of testimony before a solution was reached (verses 12-21). The whole chapter presupposes a legislative assembly in which all sides present their point of view; then a discussion develops to discover what seems to be the best solution, given all the facts and opinions. The decision might not necessarily be "true," but it would be one that the participants could "live with" until more clarity could be developed in the light of further experience. This process of argument and discussion is clearly indicated in Thessalonica where "Paul went in, as was his custom, and for three weeks he argued with them from the scriptures, explaining and proving that it was necessary for the Christ to suffer and to rise from the dead . . ." (Acts 17:2-3). The same technique was employed in Berea, where the Jews studied "the scriptures daily to see if these things were so" (Acts 17:11), and in Corinth, where Paul settled down for a while as a tentmaker and where "he argued in the synagogue every sabbath" (Acts 18:4). When Apollos came to Ephesus with his accurate but incomplete knowledge of Jesus, Priscilla and Aquila spoke up in the discussion period that followed and filled in Apollos' gaps of knowledge (Acts 18:24-26). These reports indicate that the synagogue was more of a forum than a place of formal worship. Apparently the give-and-take that went on in the synagogue was a characteristic of the newly formed Christian churches, if we can rely on the description of the church at Ephesus (Acts 19:8-11). Certainly the method of argumentation and discussion was Paul's standard technique; the book of Acts ends with him in Rome gathering people about him daily as he expounded the Scriptures "from morning till evening" (Acts 28:23).[10] The structure of the book of Romans also illustrates this method.

It takes a body of believers to develop a mentality which in turn will shape and hold a tradition. It takes debate to forge a belief system. Reality is displayed in conflict and argumentation, which when carried out to arrive at truth is perhaps our finest educational process. In the areas of our life where we care—such as politics and economics—we argue in order to hammer out our policies. If we really cared about our faith, we would argue about it—not to establish our point and expose those who differ but in order to forge the mind of faith. Our fear of argumentation probably indicates that we really fear change or that our interpersonal relations are so flimsy that they will not support an honest difference of opinion while we search for truth.

Our contemporary understanding of the New Testament assumes that the method of discussion and debate lies back of our Scriptures. In the years after the resurrection, Christians had to find themselves in relation to God's purpose as shown in the Old Testament. They also had to justify their Sunday against the Jewish Sabbath, the Lord's Supper as a celebration, their morality in relation to Jewish moral law, their freedom from food taboos in relation to Jewish ceremonial customs, their lack of concern for food offered to idols in relation to Greek practices, and so on and on as the radical freedom offered in Christ worked its way through the morass of traditions, superstitions, taboos, and legalisms which surrounded both Jews and Gentiles.

It is now assumed that as groups of believers had to face these issues in their everyday life, they developed materials to suit their needs. They collected the pithy sayings of Jesus, the parables, and the sections of Scripture that Jesus had interpreted. These materials were written out of the church's needs. To such a collection were added hymns, liturgical materials, and poems composed for use in worship. The New Testament books all reflect the particular conditions that produced them, and they have preserved for us not only the Christian tradition in its normative apostolic form but also the situation out of which various congregations hammered their beliefs.

Some of the books of the New Testament appear to be the result of what we today would call adult study groups preparing curriculum materials for a special purpose. Krister Stendahl has made a detailed presentation of a theory that Matthew's Gospel was produced by such an adult study group of Gentiles and Jews—the School of Matthew—in order to present and defend the gospel.[11] The topical arrangement and the pattern in which the story of Jesus is told suggest that it was intended as a manual for a communicants' class. Hebrews is an unusual book, rather different from the other New Testament books because it uses the Platonic notion of the imperfect present world as only a copy of the perfect real world that is beyond this life. Moule has pointed out that the exegesis in Hebrews is so subtle it presupposes a group of educated Christians who are engaged in a systematic re-examination and re-application of the Greek Scriptures in debate with non-Christians who are serious in their desire to understand the Christian faith.[12]

All of the books of the New Testament share in their testimony that Jesus Christ is God's revelation and that in him a new age has begun. But there are remarkable differences in theological emphasis and interpretation. Paul emphasizes man's inability to do anything good because of his sin, and he sees God's grace as the only answer to this problem. James, on the other hand, tends to see religion as a duty. John's Gospel has defied all attempts to explain its uniqueness in comparison to the Synoptic Gospels. The general features are easy to describe—its emphasis on the individual, the effort to relate Jesus to the creation of the world, the lack of concern for chronology, the evangelistic intention of the writer, the need to explain the work of the Spirit in Christ's absence, and so on. It is generally regarded today as a brilliant effort to proclaim Jesus Christ to the needs of a Greek audience, and it may have behind it an independent historical tradition. But in any case, it interprets the life and work of Jesus differently from the Synoptics and puts an emphasis on the believer's need to "abide" or live in Christ.

These various interpretations reflect the experience not just of the writers but also of different Christian congregations to whom they were written or by whom they were written. Such an analysis conforms to our experience in denominations—we hold to the central truth of Jesus Christ but vary widely in emphasis, polity, theology, and worship. Even a congregation of a particular denomination will have within it a wide spectrum of belief. Rather than trying to hide these differences or gloss over them as most of us do, we should expose them and make these varying opinions the substance of our discussion and sermons. It is only by such honest argument, subordinated to our common allegiance to Jesus Christ, that we can ever obtain a meaningful faith. For this process there is no substitute for the face-to-face relationship of believers who worship together and have ties of affection and common experiences.

Confronting Issues Makes Faith Ethically Alive

Fourth, the congregation makes faith ethically alive as it confronts issues. We have already pointed out that one cannot move easily from a general ethical proposition to a concrete human problem because the human problem has a reality of its own which conditions the general ethical proposition. Ethical problems of this nature were not easily solved in New Testament times. If we turn to Matthew's Gospel, we find that a person is told to turn the other cheek if slapped, and that if anyone sues one for his coat, he should let him have his cloak also (Matthew 5:39-40). But in the latter part of the same Gospel, we find: "If your brother sins against you, go and tell him his fault . . . if he does not listen, take one or two others along with you, that every word may be confirmed by the evidence of two or three witnesses. If he refuses to listen to them, tell it to the church; and if he refuses to listen even to the church, let him be to you as a Gentile and a tax collector" (Matthew 18:15-17; see also 1 Timothy 5:19). In some way we have to reconcile these two procedures for handling personal grievances; perhaps the only way we can do so is to say that the first (from the Sermon on the Mount) is an ideal that we should follow and that the second is a three-step procedure which we must follow in order to adjudicate personal differences.

The responsibility for making ethical judgments was a regular part of the congregational life of the New Testament church. Paul wrote specific instructions to the church in Corinth about personal morality (1 Corinthians 5:1-2), and he was very positive that personal grievances should not go to law courts but to the congregation for adjudication (1 Corinthians 6:1-8). Moreover, Paul's letters were, in part, advice to the congregations about how they were to handle special cases and personal morality (1 Corinthians 7:1-17). This role of the church in adjudicating personal conflicts and setting moral standards was an obligation of their particular situation. They had to interpret the Jewish law in the light of the sayings of Jesus and the new freedom into which the Holy Spirit had led them. They also had to interpret these standards, especially the sexual ethics, to converts with a pagan background. If a person joined the church and his spouse did not, what obligation did he have to her? (see 2 Corinthians 6:14). Even the matter of paying taxes became an ethical problem and had to be treated (Matthew 17:24-27). These and other practical, concrete, ethical matters had to be examined. The churches provided the human context and the human concern that made a moral norm possible. These matters were not considered the domain of the individual but of the church. New Testament Christianity was corporate, as was Judaism out of which it came. To be Christian was to be a part of the Body of Christ (1 Corinthians 12:12-28). The writer of First Timothy put the matter of morals in the church context in these words: "I hope to come to you soon, but I am writing these instructions to you so that, if I am delayed, you may know how one ought to behave in the household of God, which is the church of the living God . . ." (1 Timothy 3:14-15; see also Galatians 6:10). The instructions given were hammered out in innumerable conversations and church debates because the church—rather than the individual—was the agency for establishing and adjusting moral norms.

Many Protestant churches have in their standards a procedure for handling cases of morality and personal ethics, but these are almost universally neglected. The main objection today seems to be that morality is an individual matter. Church members seem to feel that the church has a responsibility to preach and teach the Christian code but has no right to adjudicate issues. The chief place where we get a systematic and careful attempt to discuss personal morality today is in the church school curriculum. Even there it has to be treated in a general way since printed material is unable to deal with the particular configuration of facts which makes up local conditions or with specific cases. So the church sees the slow, steady moral decline which affects every part of our society; yet, the church will become increasingly ineffective in personal morality unless we are able to reassert the New Testament role of the congregation as the place where morals are discussed and specific issues decided in the light of the facts of the case and the gospel we profess. The irony of our modern situation is that morals are discussed by our church members before and after church meetings or during the week. Moral issues do not go unnoticed in the community, and concrete cases always demand an answer. Perhaps the church was right in allowing the machinery of church courts to get rusty; too often it was used in a manner of moral self-righteousness which undermined the grace of the gospel. However, the church was wrong in allowing moral issues to become a responsibility of the individual rather than of the congregation. It is only as people face issues that are real to them in the light of God's revelation that faith can be ethically active, and it is only in face-to-face interaction with other people who share the same commitment that an inner resolve to live ethically can be developed, maintained, and clarified.

The home is often singled out as the place where personal morals are to be inculcated, and a good case can be made for the formation of character in the early years of a child's life. But to require the home to take full responsibility for moral training is to fool ourselves. Not only are many parents incapable of discharging this responsibility, but also those who are capable are often perplexed about what normative Christian conduct should be under specific circumstances in the community. Furthermore, the surrounding culture erodes the best desire of parents when they have to face concrete decisions for their children. For Christian parents the place to establish moral standards and to adjudicate between standards and specific cases is the church, where parents can share their hopes and fears in an environment of faith and can work out solutions which can be modified and adjusted to the specific, personal conditions that obtain in the family. In short, the affectional relations in the family may be effective in shaping moral character, but unless the church shapes the mind and heart of the parents, the family goals will not be different from those of the surrounding society.

When we move beyond personal morality into social ethics, we find that the New Testament faith does not provide much guidance. The reason is clear. Early Christians were not, in the main, Roman citizens, and they did not have a sense of responsibility in civil affairs. Many of them had the usual Jewish hostility to Rome and wanted no part of the Roman Empire. They paid their taxes and that was all. Even if they wanted to participate in civil affairs, the possibilities for activity by citizens were limited. Our concept of representative democracy in which a person has political channels of communication and action was unknown. Moreover, in the early years of the church there was an expectation of Christ's early return and no long-range plans were made. Social ethics were, in fact, unknown because the Christians had no conception of themselves as being capable of reforming or reshaping society. Slavery was an accepted institution. The only reaction to it on the part of Christians was to treat converted slaves as brothers in Christ, as illustrated by the letter to Philemon. The subordinate position of women was accepted even in the church (1 Corinthians 14:34-35). Now these matters are viewed differently, not merely because times have changed but because we believe the Spirit of God has brooded over the church, leading her to different positions on these matters.

But the church has not always changed, nor has the church often led in social ethics. This is tragically illustrated by the way the church has often been a laggard in helping the Negro obtain his rights as a citizen and in extending to Christian Negroes the brotherhood that should be normal for anyone who shares our faith in Jesus Christ. In race relations, as in many other areas, leaders have often been Christians, nurtured in the church, yet rejected by the church when they sought changes in the social order. This lag between prophet and institution is an old phenomenon mentioned even by Jesus (Matthew 23:29-30). The reason for the discrepancy is our reluctance to bring issues of social ethics into the congregation. Such inattention of the congregation to ethical issues is one of our most serious problems; it makes the church irrelevant to conditions which shape our lives. The church should not become engaged in partisan politics. And many international political issues are so complex there is no way a congregation can be adequately informed in order to make a judgment. But issues which affect life in general require a value judgment about the quality of human life, and this should be a normal part of the spiritual and intellectual diet of the congregation. If these issues are not a part of the congregation's life, then the church says in effect that the Christian faith does not care about, or is unrelated to, race relations, poverty, birth control, quality of public education, or other issues that shape the destiny of our contemporary life. The church must learn that there is no neutrality. To avoid a social issue is to communicate to the local believers that the Christian faith is unrelated to that particular need. To identify these issues as vital for faith and to carry on a constant study of them, searching for the will of God, is the only way to make faith ethically active.

Today we have a world-wide church with many divisions and denominations. We live in a world so interrelated and interdependent that we have to think in world terms. "The church" means the whole church everywhere—clergy and laity—where Jesus Christ is confessed as Lord and Savior. Current thinking on social issues from all sources and regions of the church must be collected and "weighed" (see 1 Corinthians 14:29). It is through such processes that we will be able to transcend our parochial restrictions, to see the needs of the church universal. At the same time, the local church must not give up her responsibility to process through mind and heart the issues which are local as well as the local part of the world issues. We said earlier that a tradition at its center is a series of values arranged in a hierarchy and that these values permeate the whole person, affecting his perception and regulating his choices. World problems of atomic warfare, racial segregation, poverty, and the like all have a place in the value structure of persons who make up our congregations. The area of concern of a congregation is the value structure of the people in relationship to these problems. That is why the issues must be discussed and deliberated within the context of the worshiping community; otherwise no significant change in attitudes will take place.

The ingredients of this process are clear. A congregation must know the Bible and must have a sense of the main themes in the Scriptures. It must have an image of God which is formed and kept clear by a review and constant reconsideration of the history of Israel and the development of the Christian church. Congregation members must also know the human situation in which they live and to which they want to address their attention.

With a knowledge of the faith and a clear understanding of the human problem, we can confront issues. There is no magic here. The process is rational. Our ability to make judgments is dependent on our general human experience and on our ability to project our decisions into the future by means of our imagination. The more we know from wide and varied human associations about the way people act and react, the motives that impel and compel actions, and the goals men seek, the more we will be able to exercise discrimination and judgment. The process is social. Our ability to make judgments is dependent upon our ability to listen to others, to blend our insights with theirs, to search for the wisdom that comes when all avenues have been explored and a common mind has been reached. Such a process seldom produces an ideal solution because it takes seriously the human situation with all of its ambiguities and weaknesses.

Ethical problems are never really solved; they have to be wrestled with over and over again as life situations change. The church is a living, human community which must constantly rework its position on ethical questions to meet new conditions. The church is not alone in her ethical struggles but trusts in the living God to give signs of his leading. This outlook creates a flexibility of mind whereby the church can move ahead with tentative decisions, always working on social problems but always open for new approaches and new solutions to ethical issues.

V

Faith and Perception

The community of believers, as we have said, is the group that fosters and gives meaning to faith by the way it worships and lives together. The individual develops his Christian self-identification by his participation in the life of a congregation. The process of self-identification goes on throughout the life span, but it is the adult groups which form and re-form a style of life to which the self is related. Adults in their various roles, especially as parents, communicate the self-image that the group forms.

This position practically equates the communication process with the life of a believing community. If we were interested only in identifying *the process* by which religious faith is communicated, we could stop our analysis here; or we might continue by an examination of various religious groups—such as the Amish, Jehovah's Witnesses, white-middle-class-Presbyterian, or any other group—to illustrate how the process works. But our main concern is how a group of Protestants can communicate the Christian faith, and this requires that the believing community be as concerned with *what* it communicates as with the method. In fact, making use of the natural socialization process assumes that what the adult group is and what it believes are the crucial elements in communication. Content and method go together when we view the communication process this way.

The group of believers, being the center of the communication process, must constantly examine the quality of its faith. Every group of believers will communicate some kind of faith which will largely determine the perceptive system of its individuals. The only issue is the quality of the faith that is communicated—the kind of world which the eyes of faith see and interpret. The church faces a strange dilemma here. We have to look backward to understand how faith was lived in the past; however, the present is not exactly like the past, so we cannot easily use history to guide the present. Yet in order for faith to have any meaning it must shape our vision so that we can see the world God wants us to see. This is not a plight we can resolve on paper; it should be in the back of the mind of every Christian as he participates in the church, because it is out of this quandary that the community of believers becomes sensitive to the leading of God's Spirit. In fact, just to pose the dilemma sharply will force the church to put first things first; it will do more than anything else to shake up misconceptions of the role of faith in the church or to replace world views that are out of date.

JOHN'S PERSPECTIVE

Our best Biblical illustration of the necessity for the church's examining itself in relation to faith and how such faith determines perspective is seen in the Gospel according to John. This Gospel came into being in and for a Greek community which did not have the Hebrew conception of time, of God's final judgment, of man as sinner, or the long tradition of the moral law. The writer either had to train his audience in Hebrew culture and then tell them the gospel story, or he could translate the gospel so that it met the needs of his congregation. John took the second alternative and showed the meaning of faith in Christ to a Greek audience. Rather than using the idea of judgment as an event which God would cause to happen in the future, John discusses the difference Jesus makes between the forces of light and darkness. Rather than starting the story of Jesus with his birth and relating his parents to a "correct" line of Hebrew ancestors as do Matthew and Luke, John connects Jesus with the beginning of the world. Rather than making an effort to tell us about Jesus with a general regard for historical sequences of events, John simply uses a few episodes as a framework on which to attach long discourses by Jesus. Rather than insisting that men first know themselves as sinners and then offering them Jesus Christ as Savior, John presents Jesus Christ in such a way that hearers will realize they are sinners.[1] Read the well-known John 3:16-21 in this light and compare this statement with Paul's discussion in Romans 1:18—6:23.

When we compare John's Gospel with the Synoptics, we are struck not only by the differences indicated above but also by the realization that the whole of Jesus' life has been interpreted from the perspective of faith in God. Edwyn C. Hoskyns says, ". . . the theme of the Fourth Gospel is the non-historical that makes sense of history, the infinite that makes sense of time, God who makes sense of men and is therefore their Saviour."[2] The "non-historical" is the belief that faith in Jesus Christ will save a person from death to eternal life, and this belief uses historical material to shape the story of Jesus. In short, the meaning of the life of Jesus is more important than the facts that make up his life.

Eduard Schweizer sums up his study of this matter by saying, "The New Testament canon contains no declarations about faith that are to be simply reproduced, and that are made correct through correct rendering."[3] There can be no such thing as a static notion of faith, because faith requires that the believers formulate a meaning to fit their situation. Such formulation must be the first charge on the congregation's time and resources. To do this we must first understand the relation of faith to the past.

FAITH LOOKS AT THE PAST

Although our faith is in God, our knowledge of what faith meant in the past is in a book. Much of the Bible—the Pentateuch, for example—was compiled centuries or (in the case of the Gospels) decades after the events took place and after the accounts had circulated in oral form for a considerable period of time. Stories are bound to change somewhat in oral form, although perhaps not as much as we would expect since the Oriental mind was trained to transmit information accurately. Back of the oral or written form of Biblical material we have the fundamental question of accuracy. Can any report of an event be accurate, or is every report also an interpretation? The problem is further complicated because all that happened in the Bible took place in a pre-scientific world; some of the material is contradictory—such as the two accounts of creation—and some is inconsistent—such as the several accounts of the crucifixion. If these problems are not enough, we also lack important data which would be of immense value to us today. For example, the Gospel records are so constructed that we are not able to work out an accurate chronology of the episodes in the life of Jesus.

Does this mean that the Bible is untrue or that we do not have a reliable basis for the Christian faith? No. But it does mean that the Bible as a book demonstrates in its own composition that it is not primarily a theological book in which we can expect to find an organized account of the Christian faith. Rather, it is a history book that describes, from the standpoint of a people who had faith in God, what that faith meant in the day in which they lived. The truly important elements were their fellowship—in the New Testament the koinonia—and the powerful bonds of belief which bound them to God and to each other. The New Testament itself makes the promise that God's presence and guidance are in the Christian fellowship. The Bible itself has this curious relationship to the church: it contains an account of the authentic apostolic tradition, as indicated in our third chapter, yet the experiencing of the apostolic tradition is normally found only in the living body of believers. The Bible gives the living community the responsibility of interpreting its own history. We shall return to this theme in the next chapter, but here we need to inquire into the way in which the body of believers views the past.

The past is gone. The only things that remain of the past are written records, monuments, buildings, artifacts, and historical events which are carried along by a living tradition. In this connection, "historical event" means an event that is still formative for the present or an event that we make formative for the present. For example, events that took place in prehistoric England are not in any significant way historical events for me today, however interesting it may be to reconstruct a life of neolithic man centered in Avebury or Stonehenge. However, the actions of King George III and the British Parliament in relation to the American colonies are a part of my history because those events led to the establishment of American independence. I may feel that the whole affair was badly managed and that the world would be better off if the English-speaking people had been able to maintain political unity; but my evaluation has nothing to do with the fact that certain events took place in the past which shaped the present in which I live. Or again, historical events may be what I incorporate from the past; that is, what I take from the past and *make meaningful* for my present. For example, the stories of Abraham in Genesis are a part of my history and as such help determine my life.

Some historians have said that the past is made up of occurrences and interpretations of occurrences, thereby showing that there are two elements in any past event. Actually, we never know a past event except by a particular interpretation. If it is a prolonged and involved event, such as a war, it will take years just to assemble the material from the opposing sides in order to arrive at a considered judgment of what may actually have happened during the war. We can know that an event truly happened and yet have no factual description on which people will agree. We can know that the Bill of Rights was affixed to the Constitution of the United States in 1791, yet our most serious social conflicts today are about the meaning of these words that were agreed to. This lack of agreement about the meaning of a past event is characteristic of history. By using the various interpretations of past events that have come to us, we can determine a rough outline of what took place and can establish the certainty that an event actually happened.

This ambiguity should not be a mystery to us. Think of any event in your life in which several people were involved and there was a conflict of interest, such as an automobile accident. That there was an acccident is clear; but no two persons can agree on just what happened or on the precise sequence of happenings that made up the accident. If the accident becomes a matter for a court trial, the lines of diverse explanation will be more sharply drawn in an effort to fix blame on the other party. If this condition is true of events that happen in the present, we can easily see how it is true of events that happened in the past.

We can, of course, discover facts from the past—facts about dates, descriptions of weapons used in war, or statements that certain events happened. But none of this is very important. We might say that the factual part of the past is the least significant for us today. At any rate, the only records we have of the past are interpretations of happenings, and until recent times no effort was made to analyze critically these records from the past.

If these summary statements are true, does it not drive us to a subjectivity wherein we have to say that history is not "true" but is only persons' opinions of what happened in the past? In a sense, this is correct. But this does not mean that the interpretation of events is wrong or false. It only means what we have observed in our own life—that events are known only by interpretation, that facts are slung in a network of narrative which makes sense through interpretation. Even stating that a certain thing is a fact indicates that it has been selected because of some intrinsic significance above the hundreds of other facts that could have been cited.

We might look at the resurrection, for example. Few people, Christians or non-Christians, would deny that the resurrection of Christ is the central event in the New Testament and the event on which the Christian faith rests. The Apostle Paul states it in these words: "Now if Christ is preached as raised from the dead, how can some of you say that there is no resurrection of the dead? But if there is no resurrection of the dead, then Christ has not been raised; if Christ has not been raised, then our preaching is in vain and your faith is in vain" (1 Corinthians 15:12-14). Yet we cannot establish the truth of the resurrection by trying to get more facts. If we had a hundred eyewitnesses with sworn accounts of the resurrection, this evidence still would not be accepted by a person today who believes that a dead man cannot come back to life. All we have and all we can ever have is a statement of faith that Jesus did rise from the dead; and the only evidence we have for it is the community of believers-in-his-resurrection and their history.

All of this raises a serious question concerning the accuracy of events in the Biblical record. Must there not be accuracy in the reporting if we are to take the record seriously? To ask this question is to misunderstand the nature of historical events. Luke, as indicated earlier, sought to date the major events in the life of our

Lord; but when his Gospel was written, the church was already at least a half-century old and the dating was for the purpose of emphasizing that the events happened, not that their truth was dependent upon the accuracy of dating. In chapter 3, verse 1, Luke says that in the fifteenth year of the reign of Tiberius Caesar, the word of God came to John. If it could be proved beyond doubt that the event occurred in the fourteenth year of the reign of Tiberius Caesar, we would simply add a marginal note to Luke's Gospel with the correct date, but such an error would have little to do with the truth of Luke's narrative. We do not defend the authority of Biblical events on the accuracy of dates or any other empirical facts. In the Old Testament, especially the older sections, we do not find historical accuracy; these writings came out of a culture that did not value "factual" reporting as much as "meaningful" narrative. The Hebrews were above all intensely concerned about the meaning of history. The vast array of archaeological data of recent years, plus the scientist's ability to date pottery and other artifacts, shows a remarkable similarity between Old Testament history and dates obtained independently of the Biblical record, but these are details. Accuracy of record is not the same as truth; accuracy has to do with facts, and truth has to do with meaning.

PRESUPPOSITIONS

Our problem, therefore, is not so much the factual nature of the Biblical record as it is the meaning that the Biblical writers supplied to the story they told. The editor of the Pentateuch put together a variety of materials in such a way that we can tell what his beliefs were. The writer of Mark used events in the life of Jesus with very little interpretive material to connect the separate stories, but the way he puts them together shows his overriding concern to show Jesus as a man of unique power.

Secular historians do the same thing. The decline and fall of the Roman Empire has never ceased to intrigue historians, but note how each of the following writers, having the same source material, found a different reason for the end of the Roman Empire. ". . . we have Gibbon attributing it to the triumph of religion and barbarism; Seeck attributes it to the destruction of the *élite*, Kaphan to physical degeneration, T. Frank to racial decline, Huntingdon to climatic conditions, such as the drying-up of the soil, M. Weber to the decline of slavery and the return to a natural economy, Rostovtzeff to a class struggle. Piganiol declares that this noble civilization was assassinated in the barbarian invasions, while Toynbee sees a failure of response to a challenge, the disaffection of the masses at a time of mortal crisis."[4] Recently, a professor of history at Cambridge University has written a new history of the Roman Empire in which he says that Rome really did not fall: it simply declined at a gradual rate. The Empire continued to select emperors and to rule a restricted geographical area for two hundred years after the so-called "fall."

When we return to Biblical interpretation, we find the problem is more involved. As we look at the varieties of Biblical interpretation, we have to face honestly three kinds of presuppositions that we bring to the Bible.

The first is in the realm of doctrine. If we believe that Jesus was a prophet and teacher but was in no wise different from Old Testament prophets except in the vigor of his obedience, then we will interpret the New Testament to make the material fit that governing doctrine. If we believe, as Thomas Jefferson did, that miracles are impossible, then we will excise all the miraculous from the New Testament and present Jesus as an ethical teacher—just as Jefferson did in his edition of the New Testament.[5] If we believe, as Bultmann does, that the Old Testament is a history of failure, then the Old Testament will be more a history of Hebrew religion than a preparation for the New Testament.[6] If we believe, as Adolf Harnack did, that religion is "the love of God and neighbour," then we will read the history of Christianity as a tendency on man's part to cover the simple direct teachings of Jesus with dogmas, ceremonies, and churchly power.[7]

A second type of presupposition is social. This was suggested in Chapter II in the idea that we tend to take Biblical stories to support modern democracy, although democracy as it is practiced in modern Western nations was unknown in the Oriental world. There are other illustrations. The divine right of kings was strongly supported by Biblical quotations, and Luther's reading of Romans has tended to make Lutheranism a strong supporter of the "two realms." Before the Civil War, theologians in the South were able to find in the Bible complete justification for slavery. When a nation is at war, many preachers can find parallels between the righteousness of their nation and Biblical passages. Capitalism as an economic system is often justified on the basis of certain parables of Jesus, such as the parable of the Talents (Matthew 25:14-30).

A third type of presupposition is personal. We often go to the Scripture with deep personal needs and select from the Scripture ideas, incidents, and affirmations which meet our particular circumstances—*without trying to relate ourselves to the God of the Bible.* The most common illustration of this is our desperate search for a way to free ourselves from the terrible pain of guilt. Since the Bible contains a vast amount of material about guilt, it is possible to find affirmations that relieve guilt feelings, such as the words, "If we confess our sins, he is faithful and just, and will forgive our sins and cleanse us from all unrighteousness" (1 John 1:9). In a similar manner, we may look for statements which relieve our loneliness, calm our fears, or offer reassurance in the face of death.

We should also observe that whether our presuppositions be doctrinal, social, or personal (or, as is most likely the case, a blending of all three) our presuppositions override our ability to interpret disinterestedly. The same critical methods of interpretation are used by unitarians, trinitarians, existentialists, and some fundamentalists, so that Biblical interpretation is more closely related to the presuppositions of the interpreter than to any particular method of interpretation.

FAITH AS A PRESUPPOSITION

To affirm that knowledge of the past, including the Biblical record, is dependent on the presuppositions we bring to the study of the past would seem to relativize everything, to make everything dependent on what we think today, or to imply that the past is powerless to communicate truth to us today. Such a blunt statement shocks us only if we have not considered the way in which events are interpreted and carried along in the stream of history. To Calvin, the Pope was the anti-Christ.[8] This view was carried along in many streams of Protestant history, including the Presbyterian Church, U.S., until 1938 when it was removed from the Westminster Confession of Faith.[9] Events recorded in the Bible were not accepted by many people of that day as having any divine importance. The Egyptians were not pleased that Moses took their Hebrew slaves away; they saw no guidance from God in that spectacular event. The Biblical narrative explains the Egyptians' reaction by saying God hardened their hearts (see Exodus 4:21; 14:8). We need not multiply examples because we know from our own experience that many people have not the slightest interest in the Bible and that, if they ever did read it, they would not take it seriously. The Apostle Paul saw that a presupposition of unbelief made the gifts of the Spirit of God "folly" and that such an unbeliever "is not able to understand them because they are spiritually discerned" (1 Corinthians 2:14).

The spiritual discernment that Paul had in mind is a function of the Holy Spirit and is related to the radical difference Paul sees between Judaism and Christianity. Let us start at the beginning of chapter 2 of First Corinthians with Paul's declaration that he "decided to know nothing among you except Jesus Christ and him crucified" (verse 2). Then he goes on to say that he is going to impart a "secret and hidden wisdom of God" (verse 7) which is "revealed to us through the Spirit" (verse 10). Then Paul has a remarkable paragraph (verses 10-16) where he points out that the Holy Spirit is a searching spirit or investigating spirit (see also Romans 8:27, the only other place where that word is used) who "comprehends the thoughts of God" (verse 11b) and that these spiritual truths are available to "those who possess the Spirit" (verse 13). He concludes with the declaration that "we have the mind of Christ" (verse 16), by which he means the Spirit that was also in Christ. This is seen more clearly in his second letter to the Corinthians, chapter 3, where he contrasts the spirit of the new covenant with that of the old covenant of Moses. Using Exodus 34:29-35 as his reference, he says that Moses "put a veil over his face so that the Israelites might not see the end of the fading splendor" (verse 13). Paul probably has in mind the idolatry that took place in the worship of the golden calf (Exodus 32:1-10) and the long tortuous history of the Hebrews as they tried to keep the law of Moses. According to Paul in this passage, the glory of God in Moses was temporary—a fading splendor that could not be corrected until the coming of the Messiah. All through that history the Hebrews had their eyes veiled by the incompleteness of the law, and even now that veil "lies over their minds; but when a man turns to the Lord the veil is removed" (verses 15-16). At this point Paul goes back to his theme that the Lord is spirit, and says that now the Spirit can remove the veil and show us the glory of living by the Spirit who comes from Christ (verse 18).

The audacity of these passages is displayed in Paul's claim that by means of the Spirit we can really know what God had in mind. Paul does not hesitate to show how differently the history of the Jews might be interpreted when one uses the presupposition that Christ was God's promised Messiah, in contrast to the presupposition of the Jews that Moses' law was all they needed in order to live obediently before God.

Let us not overlook Paul's interpretation of the reason for Moses' having a veil over his face. According to the account of Exodus 34:29-35, Moses' face shone because he had talked to God; he used the veil so that the Hebrews would not fear him when he reported to them the commandments of God. The veil heightened the effect of Moses as God's spokesman and indicated the divine origin of the law. Paul gets almost the opposite meaning out of it by saying Moses used the veil to hide from the Hebrews the fact that the law was already a "fading splendor" (verse 13). How could Paul so drastically reinterpret this passage? He could do so only because he used the presupposition that the law was inadequate and incomplete and that a new revelation had come in Christ. Paul was correct in his reinterpretation from a Christian point of view but in error in his exegesis of the narrative used; thus, we see how presuppositions can override facts in an effort to show truth and how different meanings can be supplied to past events when there is a shift in presuppositions.

The Apostle Paul believed that Jesus of Nazareth was the ful-fillment of the Old Testament expectation of a Messiah and that the church was the new Israel of God. This revelation from God ushered in a new era of freedom from the law (2 Corinthians 3:17) and created an allegiance to the Spirit of Christ (see chapter 4). Paul's whole being was dedicated to the preaching of the good news that "God was in Christ reconciling the world to himself, not counting their trespasses against them, and entrusting to us the message of reconciliation" (2 Corinthians 5:19). Earlier in this paragraph Paul said that "if any one is in Christ, he is a new creation; the old has passed away, behold, the new has come" (2 Corinthians 5:17). Although God's revelation of Jesus Christ as the New Covenant offers salvation to men by faith alone and gives a new center for history, yet the advent of Christ has not changed the Biblical way of understanding history. We are to understand history by faith. This is an affirmation of both Testaments, al-though faith in Christ causes us to read the Old Testament differ-ently, as the Apostle Paul has demonstrated.

What specifically are the characteristics of faith as a presupposi-tion for interpreting the past?

Faith Creates an Expectancy

Faith as a presupposition assumes that God is a force in, or the controller of, human events and that the observable events of life are the media through which he works. Such an affirmation raises serious questions about the sovereignty of God and the control of events. If God is in events, why does he allow wars, accidents, disease, plague, and other evils? There is no answer to this ques-tion that will fully satisfy the rational mind, nor will such a mind see any sense in a solution to the problem of sin that rests on the crucifixion of a Galilean peasant. Such an interpretation is, and has been, folly to those who want a rational explanation of life (1 Corinthians 1:18-25). But the affirmation of faith is that God has "made foolish the wisdom of the world" and that, if a person accepts Jesus as the Christ, then he will know "the power of God and the wisdom of God."

Such a view leads to an expectation in personal affairs. This expectation is the root of evangelism. "Without faith it is impossible to please him. For whoever would draw near to God must believe that he exists and that he rewards those who seek him" (Hebrews 11:6). Evangelism should be important to the church today because the gospel is the good news to sinners; if the church ever loses this emphasis, it loses the message that brought it into being in the first place. Evangelism is also important because the evangelistic impulse is the native desire to share the Christian faith. It focuses all of the past on the present in a human situation, wherein a person has to make a commitment of his life. The evangelistic situation is full of expectancy, forgiveness of sin and removal of the burden of guilt, the possibility of a new kind of life, and the hope of life eternal. A person must believe to be saved. Belief is the conviction of a person who yearns for fellowship with God.

Faith in God is also the way a person responds to events in his life. The believer expects God to be present in some form in the events that happen to him even if he can only partially understand how or why this can be true. Faith creates a way of regarding and responding to events. To a man of faith God is not a mental concept—the embodiment of beauty or, even less, the voice of conscience: he is a living reality that in some way illuminates passing events and makes his will known through these events. Faith is a way of perceiving God in the familiar, daily round of experience, accepting what we cannot change, rejoicing in the pleasures that come our way, working for goals in our community life which incorporate the spirit of Jesus, and resisting influences that corrupt and degrade human beings. All of this is done with the expectation that these events are the ones God cares about. Such an attitude creates an openness to the future, a sense that the divine reality behind events cannot be scheduled or hurried. Although we must plan our life, we must not be surprised to discover as we move along through time that the plan has to be constantly revised. Another way of putting the matter would be to say that rather than trying to achieve certain goals (for example, efficiency in home management or success in business or competence in a profession, all of which are based on a highly rational control over our life and will result in a series of achievements that might be cited in *Who's Who*), the man of faith will try to become a part of God's process in the world. He will count his success according to how well he is used in God's cause (see 2 Corinthians 12:1-13; Philippians 4:11-12).

Likewise in the wider scale of events, faith creates an expectancy that God has a destiny for the world. Reinhold Niebuhr has made the case that there is a profound difference between societies where no Messiah is expected and other societies where a Messiah is expected.[10] In the former, history is often reduced to a process of nature wherein man simply lives and dies as does all nature, or else history is swallowed up in eternity wherein man attempts by reason to ally himself with the God who is pure reason. In neither case is history considered to be a series of human events taken seriously as a means of understanding life itself. In contrast we have Israel, where there was a long expectation of a Messiah. Although the level of awareness of the coming Messiah changed in different periods of Israel's history and the meaning of "the word of the Lord" was variously interpreted by the prophets, there was kept alive the idea that God is judge, that the penalty for Israel's sin was in her history, and that the remedy for her condition would be the Messiah.

These observations lead us to note the profound difference between a church that no longer seriously expects the Messiah to return and a church that does expect an end to history with the second coming of Christ. The difference has been studied by sociologists of religion who point to the former as the denominations and the latter as the sects. The denomination has settled down to the world as it is and has sought to establish itself by the truth of its theology, the antiquity of its tradition, or its usefulness to the state in creating moral character in the young. The sect, on the other hand, is often made up of people who have been disinherited by the world. These people look forward to an end when God will right the scoreboard by judging the wickedness of the rich and mighty. The sect often resists the state and refuses to put much confidence in education or any man-made structure for improving human life. This situation is tragic because the denomination tries to live too much by its institutional power and prestige and does not exhibit enough trust in the leading of God for changing conditions in the future. The most glaring example of this lack of faith is seen in some of the expensive church buildings in our cities which were built twenty-five years ago; today they look like a silly gesture when compared to the problems the church faces in those same locations. The sect, on the other hand, while living in expectation of an early *parousia* and therefore spending only modestly on buildings and institutional structure, too often is unwilling to attempt solutions to pressing social or religious problems because the end of the world is expected soon.

The second generation of Christians in the New Testament had to face this problem, since Jesus had not yet returned as they expected. Their statement of the problem and their solution is found in Matthew, chapters 24 and 25. In brief, their eschatological view of history states that there will be an end to history but that no one knows the time, so "you also must be ready; for the Son of man is coming at an hour you do not expect" (Matthew 24:44). What, then, do Christians do while waiting for the end? The answer is found in the three parables in chapter 25. Like the five wise bridesmaids, we are to be spiritually prepared; like the man with the talents, we are to use what we have for the Kingdom; and like the nations that are placed on the right hand of God for judgment, we are to use our corporate power to serve Christ by serving our needy neighbor. We are to be in, but not of, the world. We are to plan and build but are to subordinate institutions to the common human good. We are to be as practical as possible but are to realize that our hold on life is tenuous. We are to expect God in the present and future because he has been experienced in the past, especially in Jesus Christ (John 1:18).

One of the principal functions of the practical work of the church is to create and maintain this expectancy that God is available now. And it is at this point that so much of our educational work fails. Didactic teaching puts out information in a form which allows the pupil to use it as information and then stand apart from it while he turns it over in his mind by logical processes alone; this method leaves the impression that Christianity is related to knowledge rather than to God who is at the moment a reality in the human situation. Although we generally associate didactic instruction with the lecture method, audio-visual aids or group discussion or any other method can be oriented so that the pupils deal with religion as if it were only a subject to be learned. What is needed is a prior understanding that God is known, and will be known, in contemporary affairs, as the affairs discussed in Biblical situations were contemporary affairs to the people involved in them at that time.

This creation of expectancy can be achieved in the way we tell the Bible story or relate the historical narrative and also in the way we end such presentations. If the story is told so that the listener will understand it as a prelude to what he must do about it, the expectancy is there. If the story is ended and then there is discussion to bring it into the present or if questions are asked by the teacher to force the pupils to incorporate it into present life situations, then expectancy is created. There is a parallel here with modern art. In good modern art, the artist suggests a theme or idea in such a way as to catch attention; the viewer must then fill in the form with his imagination or experience the rest of the picture within himself in order to complete the picture. So, teaching done to elucidate faith starts with the expectation that God is and that he will become real to those who "diligently seek him" (Hebrews 11:6, K.J.V.).

Faith Provides Meaning

When men of faith look to their past, they do not see a different past from that of other human beings: they see the same past differently. Faith provides a framework of meaning by which the past is interpreted and a criteria by which facts and events are selected for a description of the past.

Since the past is gone, we are not able to reconstruct it exactly as it happened. We have only information from the past which people in those days thought important enough to record or which can be inferred from the kind of pottery or other artifacts that have endured through the ages. There are many things they did not record, simply because they did not think them important or because those people did not pose the question for which certain information would be the answer. For example, we would like to know what certain birds were like four thousand years ago in order to see how they have changed; but, lacking Darwin's questions about mutation of the species, the Egyptians recorded no reliable information about birds. We are dependent for our information from the past on what persons living in the past thought was important out of the multitude of events that took place at that time; and we have that information within the thought forms of that day.

This description of the limitations which are imposed on us by the way information is preserved should not discourage us. We must go back to our basic proposition that faith is a spontaneous, instantaneous element which provides meaning for the events that happen. Men of faith in Biblical times recorded those events that were significant for their faith. If we had been historians writing between the eighth and sixth centuries before Christ, we would have recorded the battles and conquests of the great military nations which represented the finest culture of that period. We probably would not have mentioned the Hebrews, a tiny nation with little political influence or military power; and, if we did, we surely would not have recorded the judgments of the prophets about the Israelites or their neighboring countries, for these preachers did not greatly influence events, functioning rather as commentators about events. As historians during that time, we could not even have dreamed that twenty-five hundred years later all that the world would be interested in would be that tiny group of Hebrews, and that the larger, more powerful nations would be known almost entirely on the basis of how their activities affected the Hebrews. However, men of faith living in those centuries saw the political drama for what it really was and selected the important items for interpretation, demonstrating how God's will should have been incorporated within the life of the nation.

Almost everything in the New Testament was insignificant to the Roman Empire and to the historians of the day. The few brief references to Christians by Roman governors are concerned with the trouble the Christians made for the rulers. But we have the New Testament because men of faith saw that those few events were important. However, they did not assume that they were required to tell a factual story. Luke starts his Gospel by saying that many others had written narratives of Jesus and it had "seemed good" to him to write an orderly account. Luke wanted Theophilus to "know the truth concerning the things of which you have been informed" (Luke 1:1-4). John's Gospel concludes with a similar declaration, that if all of the things Jesus did were recorded, probably "the world itself could not contain the books that would be written" (John 21:25). In another place he said Jesus did many other signs "which are not written in this book" (John 20:30). On what basis, then, did John write his Gospel? The answer would be: ". . . these are written that you may believe that Jesus is the Christ, the Son of God, and that believing you may have life in his name" (John 20:31). With that purpose he selected his material, probably from a source independent of the other Gospel writers, and gave us a Gospel which reinterpreted the meaning of Christ from the beginning of time and connected Christ with the ongoing life of the church.

Within the remembered life of Jesus some events are better known and better authenticated than others, but the faith that led to their selection and use was not disturbed by some irregularities. John's Gospel gives us an example. The story of the woman taken in adultery (John 7:53—8:11) is not recorded in the oldest manuscripts we have of John's Gospel, and it is in no other Gospel; but because the story is so much in harmony with the teachings of our Lord on forgiveness, it is contained in the present versions of the New Testament. Perhaps this is one of the many events to which John referred as known to the disciples yet not incorporated in one of the Synoptic Gospels. Today, although we would like to have more of what Jesus said and did, we have only what men of faith of Jesus' time thought important for inculcating faith; and they had no way of knowing what additional interest we would have today.

This process of faith-selection of facts and events—not on the basis of external appearance, but on the ability of an event to illuminate and explain the happenings of life—should not be difficult to grasp if we use our own life as an illustration. In recalling the story of our life, we enumerate the facts of birth, schooling, family conditions in which we were raised, and success we have had in our career. But when we tell the story, we dwell on those lucid moments that were turning points, such as the experience or chance comment that led us into a certain line of work. It is these lucid moments which make the facts of our pilgrimage meaningful. Sometimes it is not until years after a short conversation or a minor occurrence that we look back and see that such an event not only determined subsequent events but also was a key experience which now floods our life with meaning. The church's memory of our Lord developed in a similar way, as a slow, careful reading of the book of Acts will show. This first history of the church is not an effort to be impartial; it is written to arouse faith in Christ by showing the divine guidance that created, sustained, and expanded the church. Although there are a lot of facts, and especially details about travel, the story is told mainly on the basis of specific events which at the time they happened may not have seemed important but which later proved to be decisive for the form taken by the church. One such event was the conversion of Saul (Acts 9:1-22). Another was Peter's vision at Joppa (chapter 10), which determined that the Christian church was not going to be a sect within Judaism.

Another way of stating the matter would be to say that history is the telling of a meaningful story. In the Bible the meaning is faith in God. This is quite different from saying that God has a plan for the world which one can find in the Bible and apply to present conditions. To see Biblical history this way would be to assume that there was a system, a law, or a set of principles that could be discovered by the rational faculty of the mind. Such a view is Greek, not Hebraic. Ever since the development of rationalism in Europe during the latter half of the seventeenth century, scholars have attempted to find some pattern in history, but none has been discovered; for Christians to say that they know God's plan would be either the height of religious arrogance or the spirit of rationalism at work. Faith sees God as an active agent in human affairs, and that is why there can be no set plan for history or for coming events, except that there will be an end to history in the future. Even a quick glance at the Bible will show that whatever plan God had for mankind was thwarted by man's sin. From the very first story of Adam and Eve through the stories of Noah and the flood, the tower of Babel, and the details of the lives of Abraham, Isaac, and Jacob, we have one continuous adjustment on God's part to meet conditions which developed because of man's sin.

In our sophisticated age, it is common to read the anthropomorphic passages in Exodus (chapters 4-9, for example), where Moses and God engage in a great deal of argument about the leadership of the Hebrews, with the kind of sympathetic smile we use when we hear children discussing affairs beyond their comprehension. Actually, there is a profound understanding of history in these passages, for the purpose of God is clear—his people are to leave Egypt and form their own nation in the promised land. This can be done only if Moses and the people have faith in God. The day-to-day problems are negotiable, so to speak, and are solved or handled as they arise. The whole subsequent history of Israel is written not from the standpoint of a plan that unfolds but rather from the standpoint of God's efforts to develop his purpose among a recalcitrant and sinful people.

The eleventh chapter of the book of Hebrews is our finest summary of this point, that faith provides meaning for the past. Here the author points out that "by faith we understand that the world was created by the word of God" (verse 3). He then traces the history of Israel from Abel, showing how faith selected the facts that were remembered in the tradition and how these lucid moments illuminated the entire history of God's people. Certainly, to include Rahab, a prostitute (verse 31) who did one act of bravery for Joshua's spies (see Joshua 2:1-21; 6:22-25; James 2:25), along with men such as Moses, who gave a lifetime of spectacular service, illustrates the way faith functions in history. That little incident was crucial for the spies and for the future of the military campaign, and that is why in later years it was given such a prominent place; at the time it occurred, it may have appeared to be a mere coincidence. And the telling of the story later not only illustrated the function of faith in the midst of common human events that were integral to a larger pattern, but also reinforced the faith in God as a covenant-keeping God, just as the spies kept their word to free Rahab and her family before Jericho was destroyed.

Faith Relates Meaning to Events

Faith is experienced and expressed in the present. The Apostle Paul in his interpretation of faith in the letter to the Romans describes true righteousness as not obedience to law but belief in Jesus Christ (3:21-31). In this discussion Paul is critical of people's effort to justify themselves by things they do (works). He recounts at some length the story of Abraham to show that Abraham was justified by his faith and not by his works, and he concludes this part of his discussion by saying to his readers that they must believe in Jesus Christ if they want to be justified (chapter 4). Paul then launches into a long and detailed explanation of what the new life in Christ is like (chapters 5-8), based on a fresh understanding of God's love. All this discussion is in the present tense, so much so that Paul moves the problem right into his own life and tells frankly how he was struggling with the law (see 7:13-25). This struggle was to continue throughout his life. Paul was able to say that "we know that in everything God works for good with those who love him, who are called according to his purpose" (8:28). He concludes his description of the life of faith with this climactic assertion of things we will always face: "For I am sure that neither death, nor life, nor angels, nor principalities, nor things present, nor things to come, nor powers, nor height, nor depth, nor anything else in all creation, will be able to separate us from the love of God in Christ Jesus our Lord" (8:38-39).

For Paul, faith was not an abstraction. It was not a museum piece to be kept alive by brushing the dust off its historical characters, such as Abraham. Rather, it was a way of living intensely and completely related to the present. His struggle with the law and with "works" was a struggle to free the present from a dead past which bound the present to absolute codes of conduct that would not, and could not, meet the needs of a changing human community. Hence, he is able to say, "The law of the spirit of life in Christ Jesus has set me free from the law of sin and death" (Romans 8:2). He translates this idea of freedom of the present in Christ in practical terms in chapters 12-16.

If we go back to the suggestion made earlier in this chapter—

that education should be considered as being closely related to evangelism—we can see how important it is to identify faith with the present. Evangelism has no meaning unless it is the evangelization of persons in the present. The art of the evangelist is seen in his ability to bring the meaning of Jesus Christ to a particular person, helping that person to accept Christ as Lord and Savior and to understand what his new life in Christ will mean in the specific problems he will face. Belief is meaningful only in the present, although it can bring from the past all kinds of illustrations, as the author of Hebrews, the Apostle Paul, and the writer James do. If we assume that education in the church is primarily for the purpose of inculcating faith in Christ, then—like the evangelist—we must focus our past on the present.

Another way of exploring this notion that faith is operative in the present is to consider the role of prayer in the life of a Christian. Prayer is faith in action. As a person believes, so he prays. If faith has little meaning, prayer is sporadic, formal, and often an expression of magic, i.e., an effort to manipulate divinity for one's own private problems. The man of faith prays spontaneously as an expression of his thankfulness for the gift of grace he enjoys, for the forgiveness of his sins, and for the guidance of God's Spirit in the problems he is facing. Prayer, to have any significance, must be related to those events that impinge directly on one's daily life.

The present is situational.   Faith is the factor which interprets the past; but since it is experienced in the present, faith is always situational. That is, faith is significant only to the extent that it is vitally related to what a person is struggling with and praying about now.

If we turn to public affairs and consider the political situation of a town or state, we see clearly how involved and complicated such matters are. Only in textbooks are the elected officers of a municipality treated in the abstract with neat lines of authority flowing from one officer to another and with an explanation of the balance of power which makes it sound rational and effective. It cannot be assumed that any plan works the way the official document describes it. Rather, the plan is a part of the "situation," and we judge the human beings involved by common sense based on experience plus our appraisal of how we would act under similar circumstances. The mayor of a town, for example, is of a certain age. If he is young, we may wonder if he has further political ambitions or if he is economically independent enough to avoid feathering his own nest while he is mayor. If he is old, we wonder if he is wise or senile or is creating a political machine he can use to favor his family and friends; or, on the other hand, we may be convinced that because of his age, he is reasonably free from personal interest and is genuinely concerned about building a better community. When we add personality traits, health, vocational experience, and other characteristics to all that we know about the mayor, then see him in relation to other leaders, and then observe them working with specific community problems, we begin to understand what the "situation" is. The situation is a combination of facts and conditions in an ongoing stream of human affairs; that is why so many of the solutions to our political and economic problems are adjustments or compromises.

I saw a city council, for example, face the situation of placing truck contracts. Offhand, this would seem easy—the council should set forth the specifications of the trucks they want, advertise for bids, and accept the lowest bid. But in this town there were the agencies of two powerful automobile manufacturers, each producing trucks and each agency being owned by a civic-minded citizen of the town. Under the circumstances, the council developed a system of writing specifications so that the truck business was rather equally divided between the two agencies in their town. That was a simple problem solved by simple strategy. Other problems reach further back into the moral structure of the community or forward into a vision of what the community is to become, and many more factors have to be considered. For example, should a community provide recreational leadership for adolescents in the summer? It is impossible to answer a question like that without knowing the community. It might be answered "yes" in some areas and "no" in others. Or, if we move our proposition over into the courtroom and pose the question of whether an eighteen-year-old boy should be sent to prison for stealing a car, we could likewise say that under one set of circumstances the question should be answered "yes," whereas under another set of circumstances it probably should be answered "no."

But whether the situation is buying trucks, planning a recreational program, deciding on the destiny of a teen-age thief, or trying to decide on one's child's educational experience, the circumstances require that the decision be made in the light of very concrete, specific factors which make up the situation. What is truly present for us is that about which we must make decisions. So, there is always an urgency and excitement about the present that causes us to function as a total person; whatever faith we have is automatically a part of the decision we are called upon to make.

When we look at all the factors in a situation, or all the factors we can see in a situation, we become conscious of how little effective control we have over events as they take place. We might arrange the effectiveness of our control of events on a continuum from thoughts that occupy our mind to world affairs and observe that as we enlarge the area of consideration, the area of our control is lessened. We can, to a high degree, control our thoughts. This does not mean that we completely control our thoughts; for our unconscious mind, biological instincts, and needs all have a way of making themselves known to our consciousness, triggering thoughts and habits that we have difficulty handling. But in comparison to controlling anything outside ourselves, we can control our thoughts.

Part of the intrigue the human mind has with mathematics is the almost complete control the mind has in manipulating figures and in using these abstract symbols to represent and then control processes in nature. A. N. Whitehead said, "It must have taken ages for the human race" to get to the place where people could abstract numbers from what the numbers represented and then by pure reason manipulate the numbers by themselves.[11] However, once that was done, man had something he could control. But the minute we leave abstract reasoning, of which mathematics is an illustration, we begin to lose control. If we move outside the self to the family, we can exert a measure of control over events; but seldom do members of a family conduct themselves as either the father or the mother desires. When we move on to national affairs, we are even more conscious of limitations. A great depression sweeps over the land and no person or combination of persons seems able to stop its devasting influence. An assassin's bullet takes the life of a president and thereafter national events proceed in a different direction. If we move to the international sphere, we have to become even more modest in our claims for control. Tolstoi in his *War and Peace* is in part debunking the idea that great men, especially generals, control events under their command; he shows in several places that the men in command did not know what was going on in battle and therefore were not really in command, although they continued to make plans and to issue orders as if they were. The same must be said of national leaders today. The leader of a great nation cannot possibly know all that is going on in the international affairs for which he has responsibility. The source of what information he has is usually biased because his advisers, being human, cannot help having their own interpretation of the meaning of events on which they are working. National leaders have to respond not only to what other nations do but also to what they think the other nation means by what it is doing.

It is characteristic of the present to be sharply conscious of the range of actions which lies beyond our effective control; this is why the present is always characterized by a certain amount of anxiety. We know the best-laid plans of mice and men go awry because of conditions, accidents, and events beyond our control. From previous experience, we know that there is an element of uncertainty, even crisis, in the most ordinary activity. A drive to the grocery store can be uneventful; but it can also be the trip in which we have an accident, the occasion of meeting a friend who starts us on a new line of action, or the time we buy a magazine that changes our attitudes about the rights of minority racial groups. Our anxiety is often increased by some decision we must make, the results of which may not be clear for years after we have made the decision. For example, a person may have to make a vocational decision, and he may not know for five to seven years later whether that decision was proper for his situation.

By pointing out our limitation on the control of events in the present, we also indicate that we cannot fit events into a rational pattern. This is not to deny that for many people life on the surface has gone according to their expectation, retirement came on schedule, and annuity funds paid off as promised. It would be hard to believe that these people in their deeper personal longings and desires found life unfolding exactly as they anticipated. There is no way we can completely reconcile an individual's personal needs and egotistical impulses with social regulations and laws that in some ways restrict personal freedom for the benefit of corporate good. If we look at life on the surface in the United States—which has enjoyed a remarkable period of stability and prosperity in the last generation—we can say that life for many people has been generally as they planned it. Even these people would be quick to say that the future may not be as the past. One can easily see that general inflation could become runaway inflation and wipe out the value of annuities within a few years. Then, too, we all know that accidents and disease do not appear on schedule. So, when we move outside the personal realm to the wider activities of life, we see how limited is our rational control. Our reason says that if we did not spend approximately seventy-five percent of our national budget on wars (past, present, and future), we would have money to clothe, house, feed, and educate not only the people in our nation but to give more generously to other nations as well. Our reason says that if all our political leaders were honest, we would have better government. Our reason says that if our children were lovingly educated and had stable home influences, they would develop into responsible adults. Our reason says that if parents in underprivileged countries would limit the size of their families, there would be enough food for the children already born. There is no need to continue in this vein, for we know that the "ifs" in the above sentences are not attainable.

When we observe the situational aspect of the present, we cannot help being struck by the ambiguity of human actions. We lived through World War II in which there was enormous suffering and wholesale death, yet the war so stimulated research that within a few years medical science was capable of new cures, and the application of new knowledge in the physical sciences has measurably improved general living conditions. During that war, President Harry Truman made a decision to drop the atomic bomb on two Japanese cities because he thought it would hasten the end of the war; while it probably did have this effect, the action also set the scientists of other countries in feverish motion to develop a similar weapon. So, today the chances of an atomic war are increased as each nation produces atomic weapons. Each new major technical development brings social repercussions, both good and bad; and technical developments in themselves change our way of life. The development of the automobile is a convenient example of technical development. We could hardly imagine life without the convenience and efficiency of the car, and we would not want to give up the vast transportation system that the car has created. Yet we must also note the large number of persons killed and injured daily in automobile accidents. Also, the car has become a problem for teen-agers because their personal freedom has been greatly increased by their ability to leave the community where they are known and go to other communities where they are not known and where there is ineffective supervision. The same ambiguity exists in relation to all technical developments.

Herbert Butterfield uses the phrase "the delicate texture of history" to express this idea. He suggests that it would be possible for a few microbes in Washington to cause a disease among political leaders that could determine who would be the master of Europe.

> The texture of history is . . . as light as gossamer, light as the thought of a person merely thinking it, and its patterns seem to change as easily as the patterns of wind on water. When we look back upon the past we see things fixed and frozen as they happened, and they become rigid in our minds, so that we think they must always have been inevitable—we hardly imagine how anything else could have happened. But when we look to the future, while it is still fluid, we can hardly fail to realise its unspeakable liquidity.[12]

Situations lead to the future. The situational aspect of events does not mean that the situation controls our actions or our ethical judgments. There is a "situation ethic" proposed for Christians today which reduces the ethical problem in every situation to an answering of the question, "What is the requirement of love in this situation?" Every situation in this system becomes a case in itself, unrelated to general principles.[13]

We use the term "situation" in a much broader sense to mean not only the details of the specific case, event, or group of events but also the history that made the situation what it is and the future results of our actions in relation to the event. Situation in this sense brings into the discussion-making process a lot of factors other than the requirement of love. When we look at any human situation through the eyes of faith we not only see the facts and forces that are at work, but also feel anxious and perplexed about the decisions we must make, because we realize that we do not have rational control over the outcome and that ambiguity lurks everywhere.

This openness to the future is an important way of saying that God is always leading his people into the future and that we must project our decisions about present situations into that future. This perspective of faith is applicable in two areas of the believers' life: first, the situations they face as a community and, second, the way they train themselves to see the meaning of events in their personal lives.

The community of believers moving along in a stream of history is constantly faced with decisions about their life as a group and their relation to the world. What they do about events that happen is a demonstration of what faith means to them. If they meet situations as they arise and believe that God's Spirit is in the situation, they must be open to a future that may prove their decisions wrong. But being open to the future is a tremendous educational experience. It conditions the way we make decisions and it requires that we review each decision as time moves on, adjusting ourselves to new conditions and allowing ourselves to be teachable.

The classic statement of this faith-perspective comes from Gamaliel. When Peter and the apostles were arrested in Jerusalem, the high priest and the council were so enraged at Peter's reply to their order that the apostles quit preaching ("We must obey God rather than men"), that many councilmen wanted them killed. But Gamaliel, an honored teacher of the law, saw the whole thing differently. He told the council to remember other troublers of Israel, such as Theudas and Judas, whose preaching came to nothing. "So in the present case I tell you, keep away from these men and let them alone; for if this plan or this undertaking is of men, it will fail; but if it is of God, you will not be able to overthrow them. You might even be found opposing God!" (Acts 5:38-39).

That same faith-perspective must be used today when a congregation faces events in the community. The members must plan a course of action in the light of their faith, but they must be open to the leading of God in the way the events turn out. Too often we make a decision to settle a matter rather than opening up the matter for further consideration and opening up ourselves to learn from the results of our decision. Real congregational learning can come only as faith relates meaning to contemporary events and then ponders the results as a test of understanding.

The second area is the way Christians train themselves to see the events of their personal lives. Adults train themselves by their interaction with each other and through the study programs in the church. Too often faith is restricted doctrinally to forgiveness, so that we think of faith in Christ only in relation to our sins. But here we are considering faith as a way of seeing all the events of life. Faith is a description of a relation to God who leads us, urges us, and sustains us as we move through new experiences. We cannot be confident about the outcome because we do not know how God is using our experiences for ourselves or for others. We have to experience the mood of Abraham and go out to our adventures without knowing exactly where we will end (Hebrews 11:8); like Moses, we endure "as seeing him who is invisible" (Hebrews 11:27); or like Paul, who knew what it was to be free from the demands of sin, we see that the Christian "might walk in newness of life" (Romans 6:4).

Contrast the "open future" mood of the previous paragraph with the kind of Biblical interpretation we find in much of the curriculum of our church schools. Often the materials are written as if everything was predestined to turn out the way it did. Theologically, that may be true, but to teach the Bible as if everything was predetermined robs it of the human factors that connect it with our life. Rather, we must transmit the Biblical narratives so that these past events will appear to us as our human situations appear today. We know our present and future are uncertain. We are anxious about the decisions we must make, about the results of the decisions, and about all the uncontrollable factors which can change our life from day to day. The more important the decision, the more anxious we are about the outcome; and the more people involved and the more momentous the occasion for shaping the future, the more our whole being is concentrated on the outcome of our decision.

The story of Jesus is an important case in point. Many children going through the average church school arrive at the crucial age of adolescence with one of two motifs in mind. One motif is the divine figure of Jesus who had no temptations, sufferings, doubts, fears, or death in the same way that they will have these experiences. Another motif is Jesus the master teacher who said some wonderful things that, if followed by everyone, would bring peace and happiness. Neither of these motifs is true; both have been denied by the church for thousands of years, yet we still have them. We seem not to be able to present Jesus in such a way that an adolescent can identify with him as a man who did have temptations, doubts, uncertainty about his future, and a real death, and whose life is a record of how his faith led him on to fulfill the will of God.

Perhaps we should not be so concerned that children learn the whole plan of salvation as that they experience the life of Jesus episode by episode, with a focus on the dramatic elements in the situations he faced and a consideration of how his life would have gone *if* he had done or said something different. Such use of the imagination would unlock the Bible stories from fixed theological presuppositions and allow them to stand as accounts of people who displayed faith in decisions about life situations which are somewhat like our situations. Then we will be able to read the Bible more as a casebook of what happened when people lived their faith than as a textbook of what we are required to believe.

VI

Faith and Values

The third natural process in the transmission of tradition is the formulation of a system of values within a person by means of rewards and punishments internalized in the conscience. The mechanism of conscience—how it is established, the stages of development, the way guilt is precipitated within and handled by the self, and the role of shame in guiding behavior—is one of the most important areas for practical theology to investigate. We know very little about the exact way a person's conscience is developed in relation to the Christian faith or about the way this process can be guided, although we know that conscience as it operates within a value structure is the most powerful regulator of human conduct.

Our present task is to discuss the way the believing community should go about the task of developing a value structure or, more specifically, how it will determine the content of Christian conscience. It is of the nature of values that they have to be assayed as they are passed on. Some are reinforced, others modified, and some abandoned. Even if we pass on the values as we received them, the child will ask, "Why?" We are forced to give a reason, though it may not be a meaningful one. Most often, the reason we give is vague—such as, "That's the way we do it," or "Because I say so." However, the meaning is clear to the child: he is expected to absorb and follow the way of life presented to him. The word "tradition," as Outler has said, should be associated with these "acts" of transmission because it is in the hundreds of little events that tradition becomes meaningful and alive to both the transmitter and the receiver.

Values, as noted earlier, are the product of social interaction and represent what a group of people think desirable. Values are, therefore, always in flux depending on the tradition to which the group adheres and the specific configuration of social events which the group faces. In a rather static, nomad culture such as that found in the patriarchal period of the Old Testament, values changed very little; but in the kingdom period, much of the controversy between the prophets and the political leaders was about the values Israel should have. In our day of rapid social change due to advanced technology, our values are undergoing intense scrutiny and modification.

Because values are related to changing social conditions, arise out of group interaction, and express what is desirable in human behavior, we who want to communicate the Christian faith must be deliberate in appraising our values. Adults are guided in evaluating their values through their interaction with each other, especially in the informal relationships in which they engage. These specific events they are facing demand their attention and action, usually after advice and help from their friends. It is the subject matter of this dynamic, normal, interactional process that we must bring to the center of our thinking and must relate to our religious heritage. Under ordinary circumstances the contemporary values of the Christian faith are hammered out by the individual members of the congregation as they attempt to interpret the past in general and the Bible in particular in relation to the events of their lives.

This intense interactional process is described in the fourth chapter as confronting issues to make faith ethically alive, but the approach is different. The community of believers makes ethical decisions as it creates events and reacts to events; but, in that sense, the approach is a problem-solving one, with the specific problem determining the solution which must be worked out. The matter before us now is the other way around. How do we interpret the tradition that has been transmitted to us so that we can consciously form the values that are desirable? Our Christian tradition includes far more than ethics, and that is why we must constantly return to the tradition—specifically to the Bible—to get our bearings.

THE PROBLEM OF INTERPRETATION

How shall we interpret the Bible in the practical work of the church? The standard problems are well known. Written in ancient languages, the Bible must be translated; since translations are interpretations, it is difficult at the outset to know precisely what the author of the book intended. The cultural setting is foreign to our experience, so idioms and ideas have to be explained in order for us to get some workable notion of what the writer was saying to his audience. The literature of the Bible comes out of a prescientific, Eastern mentality which was at home with myth, poem, legend, story, and parable. Much of this material is strange to our modern rational mind. In addition to all this, the Bible was written for adults; yet in our practical work we must attempt to use it also with children and youth.

Biblical interpretation brings our whole being into focus. It is a procedure which unites all of our learning with our desires and hopes. In the final analysis, the sentiments of a person usually control the rationale in interpretation. Sentiments are not emotions alone; they are also powerful in governing our reason. The Bible deals with the meaning of life, death, moral conduct, sin, salvation, God's judgment, and the final end of the world. When we put ourselves in relation to these Biblical topics, we find that we cannot be neutral for our own life is at stake. Whatever meaning we have been able to derive from life is challenged, confirmed, or confused by the Bible. Seldom are we able to do the one thing the Bible would ask us to do—to be open to the Spirit of God as we read a passage—because we approach the Bible with a prior interest or even a preconceived answer to the question the Bible poses. We must not assume that having a prior interest is detrimental to our interpretation; rather, we must see that our prior interest is the motivation for study. We should not assume otherwise. The issue is "Can we go to the Bible with our twentieth-century scientific, speculative type of reasoning, with our American middle-class Protestant denominational background, and with our own personal interests and still be open to the Spirit so that we may be led into our faith rather than confirmed in our predisposition?"

Our next problem is "What do we want to transfer from the Biblical record across two thousand years?" We have usually transferred doctrines or beliefs, moral precepts, a description of man's condition of sin, or illustrations of religious experiences. But the Bible is not primarily a depository from which we are expected to extract these things; it is first a record of a society of believers who put their trust in God. The results of that trust—and, at times, lack of trust—are recorded in the Bible.

That is why the Bible as a book is not organized chronologically, is not logically consistent from one book to another, has time gaps of hundreds of years during which no material is recorded, contains a vast array of literary forms including diverse accounts of the same events, and even has some material that is mainly of general human interest with no special religious connotation, such as the Song of Solomon and the book of Proverbs. Moreover, during the eighteen hundred years or more spanned by the material in the Bible, all of these matters changed under varying conditions; the only constant identity we have is the God in whom the people placed their faith. But the God of the Bible is seldom discussed in abstract terms. He is described primarily in terms of historical events, with stories, parables, and songs used to round out the conception of God and to communicate his meaning to contemporaries. We have to learn to think historically in order to interpret the Bible. Thinking historically is not the same thing as knowing Biblical history: to think historically is to examine the past so that it can be used in a meaningful way for the present.

SYMBOLS

Recall that we started our analysis with a discussion of tradition. We pointed out that a baby is born into a tradition in the sense that he is of a certain color, nation, race, class, religion; all of the values related to these circumstances are blended together in the parents and other adults who nurture the child. The baby appropriates their values and world view and develops his self-identification in culture. He does not know himself apart from what his culture has given him, although he may to some extent modify or change his social inheritance. The child does not come into self-awareness and then discover culture; he finds and defines himself in a particular culture. He does not look around him with fresh and innocent eyes and begin to make sense out of his environment; rather, interpretations of his environment are given him as he experiences it. He does not see the world directly: he sees the world already structured, labeled, and explained. If he is to discover a different world, he will have to do it when he becomes mature, and then only with the greatest of difficulty. Because all of this is done from infancy on through childhood by parents who love him and care for him, the appropriation of their way of seeing and living is built deep into his personality—partly unconsciously —and it permeates his whole being. Perhaps this is why a child can be raised to believe almost anything.

Culture is interpreted to the child through symbols, of which language is the principal vehicle. Language itself—the vocabulary, grammar, and inflection—is an expression of culture and reflects some of the major characteristics of the culture. Hebrew, for example, is a verbal language with an emphasis on specific occurrences in contrast to a noun-centered language with its interest in universals.[1] Although language is itself a symbolic process, it also has the power to transmit symbols, and much of our religious tradition is stated symbolically. When we say, "Christ is the lamb of God that taketh away the sin of the world," we have used a symbol to express one of our most precious and profound truths. But we need to explain that symbol. In an area where sheep are known, it would not be necessary to explain the docile nature of the sheep; but it may be necessary to explain the idea of sacrifice, and it would certainly be required to show how sins we have committed two thousand years after Christ's death could be "taken away." Once all this is done, the phrase is full of meaning.

Explaining the symbol connects the past with the present, but it also puts the human experience in a structure of meaning so that the person who receives the explanation receives a particular view of God and man. Symbols define and explain the human situation simultaneously, and this is why they are related to—and a function of—the value system of the tradition. A symbol, like a value, is not neutral. It says something clear-cut about the human situation, and it does it in a way to gain adherence. Symbols, being related to culture and especially to language, have a way of changing over the years. Certain symbols wax in importance; others wane; and still others hardly change at all, indicating that they are central to a human experience which does not vary from age to age. The symbol of sacrifice for sins remains the same all through the Bible and is still in widespread use today. The symbol of the Ark of the Covenant (Exodus 25:10-22), although important to our understanding of the development of the Hebrews, is not alive as a symbol to Protestants today because it has been superseded by the new covenant in Christ. Baptism, on the other hand, although practiced by the Jews for adult converts in the first century (Luke 3:3; Mark 1:5), was taken over by the Christian church; and from Pentecost on (Acts 2:38-41) it came to mean in Christianity a participation in the death and resurrection of Jesus (Romans 6:3-6; Colossians 2:12; 1 Corinthians 12:13).

Our interest in symbols is in their power to communicate. A symbol is an object or a mental image which represents what cannot be seen. A symbol makes human experience intelligible and communicable, and it does both simultaneously. Although some symbols are self-evident, most of them arise out of a living tradition and are most meaningful in that tradition, sometimes being meaningful only in that tradition. For example, because I am a Western Protestant, I do not respond to the cow as a symbol of anything sacred, but it does represent something sacred to the Hindu in India. Culture, as we said earlier, develops symbols which both define and explain life and are the means of transmitting the culture to each succeeding generation. It is important to note that symbols are pre-eminently the language of religion because they are able to connect an everyday experience or object with the tradition's understanding of reality and to do it by means of a mental image that is easily understood.

Biblical symbols have their origin in human situations in which revelation occurs. Symbols have to be taught. Most often this is done spontaneously and naturally by the same informal process by which the child is taught customs, use of clothing, the place of work, sex differentiation, and other matters that are automatically communicated within a culture. Other symbols have to be explained. For example, when the Hebrews had passed over the Jordan into the Promised Land, Joshua ordered a monument of stone to memorialize the guidance of God; he told the people that in days to come their children would ask, "What do these stones mean to you?" And they were to reply that God had guided them safely over the River Jordan (Joshua 4:1-7). Perhaps a better illustration is found in Deuteronomy 6:20-25, when Moses instructed the people regarding the Commandments because he saw that the Commandments, although self-explanatory, carry no motive for obedience. "When your son asks you in time to come, 'What is the meaning of the testimonies and the statutes and the ordinances which the LORD our God has commanded you?' then you shall say to your son, 'We were Pharaoh's slaves in Egypt; and the LORD brought us out of Egypt with a mighty hand . . .' " Moses continued by showing what God had done in the Israelites' history, and their memory of that event was the motive for keeping the Commandments. The Commandments are symbolic of morality, but the Exodus was symbolic of God's favor and guidance; the two had to go together, lest the Commandments become a burden (see also Exodus 20:2).[2]

The great Old Testament symbols were related to their historical tradition. Names were symbolic, such as "Emmanuel," meaning "God is with us" (Isaiah 7:14). The name for God was so sacred that it was not pronounced. Great leaders became symbolic, so that the name Abraham came to mean "the nation" (Genesis 17:5-8; Romans 4:1-5; James 2:21). Moses became synonymous with the Law (John 1:17), and David was remembered with the glories of the kingdom (Mark 11:10). We have mentioned the Ark of the Covenant as an Old Testament symbolic object. We can remember also the pillar of cloud for divine guidance (Exodus 13:21), or personal objects such as phylacteries to help the wearers remember service and obedience to God (Exodus 13:16). Certain places became symbols, too—such as Sodom for immorality (Isaiah 1:10), Egypt for slavery (Exodus 20:2), and Jerusalem for the holy city (Revelation 21:2).

Common experiences were used so constantly to illustrate spiritual truths that they became symbols which were taken over by the Christian church and are widely used even today. Symbols having to do with sheep, for example, were connected with Jesus as he became known as the Good Shepherd (John 10:1-18). The underlying ideas related to sheep are used today in defining the role of a bishop: he carries a shepherd's staff, both as a symbol of his office and to remind him of his duties. The Old Testament is full of allusions to the vine. This figure of speech was picked up by John to illustrate the relationship between Jesus, God the Father, and the believers (John 15:1-11). Most of the symbols in the New Testament are taken from the Old Testament and are applied to Jesus and the church. Jesus is shown to be a prophet (John 6:14), priest (Hebrews 4:14—5:10), and king (Matthew 21:15; John 18:36-37).

The major symbol of the Christian faith is the cross. It has a variety of meanings associated with salvation (Colossians 2:13-14), with crucifixion (Galatians 6:14), with the power of God (1 Corinthians 1:18), with the uniting of the Gentiles with believing Jews (Ephesians 2:11-16), with the way a Christian should live (Luke 9:23-27), or as a symbol of the goodness against which some rebel (Philippians 3:17-20). Moreover, the idea of crucifixion is central to Christian behavior. Paul tells the Galatians that they should crucify the passions and desires of the body in order to live more fully by the Spirit (Galatians 5:24-25; see also 2:20). The cross—Christ's sacrifice for sin—provides the focus for the believing community and inspires ethical conduct as it is re-enacted in the communion celebration. The most powerful and central symbol of all our Christian life, it re-enacts in contemporary life the meaning of the incarnation. It connects the person with the past, it defines and absolves the sin of man, it relates the person to the believing community, and it lifts up the possibility of a finer, more noble existence in spite of the power of sin and evil (1 Corinthians 10:16-18; 11:23-34).

There are other symbols throughout the Bible that are more clearly related to man as a psychological being than to the particular history of the Hebrews. The symbol of the snake in the Garden of Eden (Genesis 3:1-7), the use of colors—such as white for

cleanness or goodness (Isaiah 1:18), the use of darkness to suggest evil (1 John 1:5-7), the offering of first fruits (Exodus
34:22), the golden calf (Exodus 32:1-6), the various beasts in
the book of the Revelation (see chapters 12 and 13, for example),
and circumcision (Genesis 17:10-14) are all examples of symbols
which have their origin in man's psychological make-up and which
appear in many traditions in widely separated countries. These
symbols are used in the Bible to illustrate Biblical themes and are
just as valid as the symbols that grew out of Israel's history; but
they are not unique, and the faith of Israel—though partially explained by these symbols—does not rest on them.

It would be strange if symbols natural to man were not included
in the repertory of Biblical symbols, for a truthful recording of
human experience would certainly include them. However, more
important is the observation that Biblical religion is characterized
by its earthiness, its frankness about man's passions and the dark,
subterranean influences that pull the self into tragic situations.
These elements in man are not to be denied. They crop out in
symbols of the snake and of the young bull, and Biblical religion
deals with these forces in man as well as with those which develop
out of his historical circumstances.

THE IMAGE OF GOD

The symbols which came from historical occurrences were the
ones which made Israel and formed the Christian church, so we
have to go back to our discussion of the nature of Biblical history
to find our key to interpretation. To think historically we have to
examine the past so that it can be used meaningfully in the present.
To do this we have to start with the events of the past we have
under observation. We must reconstruct the mentality that informed the era in which the specific events occurred. To do this we
have to know the language used, the social and political conditions
that obtained, cultural values, world view, climatic and natural
resources which surrounded the people. All of this is available to
some extent through normal historical research, including the use
of science to help us date artifacts.

It is at this point that we often make our first major error in
Biblical interpretation. In our eagerness to find meaning in the

accounts, we often grasp an idea or words which appear significant to us today without knowing the meaning the words and ideas had for the people who used them. One of the tragic illustrations of this inaccurate method is the way we use the Ten Commandments. Our usual procedure is to move from the words of a commandment directly to our day; the result is a moralistic interpretation which makes our auditors feel guilty without necessarily motivating them to appropriate the moral law. I have indicated earlier that the Ten Commandments have to be interpreted within the context of the loving-kindness of God who gave the covenant; this is shown by the context in which we find the Commandments in Exodus (20) and Deuteronomy (5). In our Christian era we have to interpret all of these commandments in the light of our Lord's teachings. A specific illustration of misinterpretation is the way the sixth commandment has been used to justify pacifism: such a view was unknown in ancient Israel.

Another illustration is the misuse of the story of David and Jonathan (1 Samuel 18-20). We often use parts of this story in our church schools to show the friendship between the two young men. We generalize on the beauty and desirability of friendship and end with an exhortation to appreciate our friends and be loyal to them. The moral we draw from this early phase in David's life is certainly a valuable sentiment, but do we do justice to the Bible by this kind of interpretation? The friendship is there, certainly; but the story shows—even more clearly—jealousy, the odd vicissitudes of history, the mixture of bitter and sweet in human ventures, and the ambition of David to be king in spite of Jonathan's right to the throne. To understand the story fully, we would first have to know the mentality of the era in which the story was lived. The friendship between the two army lieutenants would be an important factor, but only one factor, in David's rise to power in Saul's army. By extracting a lesson on friendship we find something that makes sense to us today, but we lose a true understanding of history which we desperately need.

If we first attempt to discover the mentality of the period we are observing and also to find as accurate a description of the event as is possible from the materials available, we are then in a position to understand the Biblical material. The great Biblical symbols are all fixed in history. We cannot appropriate them without developing our ability to think historically. We have to imagine what the situation was like and then we will learn that Biblical revelation came through particular human events, some of which were quite ordinary, but all of which were observed and understood within the experiences of human beings like ourselves. The experiences should remain connected with the event in order to convey the truth of God, because God's truth is often particular to the event in which it was revealed; to strip it of its historical setting is to run the danger of losing the reality of the God of the Bible.

Biblical history is the framework in which we see God. What is transferred is not history as such but the image of God we see in the material of history, a mental picture created by God's activity in history. We study the Bible in order to discover the image of God which can be brought through the centuries and across cultural differences to our day. The only way we can get an authentic mental picture of God is through Biblical history. Most of the heresies of the Christian religion have developed when the whole Bible was not taken seriously; and, contrariwise, the great periods of reform, of missionary enterprise, and of renewal have come to the church when men went to the Bible to recover an authentic image of God. Ernest Wright has stated the matter in these words:

> The biblical event, then, is an occurrence in the realm of human living which structures life, which produces in the community of the individual and in the individual himself a new conformation or *Gestalt*. The event brings into being, and is remembered in such a way that it continues to form, a powerful *image,* a creative image, which cannot be reduced to an abstraction, whether as principle, law, grace, or forgiveness. Jesus Christ, who was born, who suffered, and who died under Pontius Pilate, is recalled as a real person in a particular history. His image or picture as an actual person is the creative center of the Christian's life. To possess that image is to be "in Christ," to follow Christ, to take up my cross as he carried his, *to become involved in my history as he was in his.* Christ is the historical event—in this instance a person with a history—who forms a powerfully creative image which would restructure the self in history to conform to him.[3]

This quotation brings out the objective nature of Biblical revelation. Something happens which forms and interprets life around a mental image of God. To the Christian the most powerful of these events is the resurrection. If one wants to see how the image of God behind the resurrection event structured the life of the early Christians, he has only to read the book of Acts to observe how the apostles were shaped and the church was formed in the light of that conception of God. There are, of course, other episodes in the life of Jesus which had their part in describing the nature of God, such as the arrest-trial-crucifixion events, the temptations, the encounters with Pharisees, Sadducees, Zealots, Roman soldiers, and ordinary people. It is the Biblical description of what Jesus said and did in specific situations that gives us a clear image of the nature of God. This is what incarnation means. Words which abstract and condense meaning—such as "God is love"—do not have as much power to communicate as a living demonstration of what love means.

Israel knew God through specific bits and pieces of her history which shaped her image of God. Indeed, her image of God was so related to history that Israel preserved the history in story and song in order to keep the image of God. This image was Israel's mental portrait of the holy; and the people kept coming back to that mental picture to test the adequacy of their religious faith. We must not think of "image" as a vague, ghostlike impression on the mind. Rather, the image is sharply etched in the mind by historical events. The receiver of revelation was able to convey this sharpness of the image of God only by the description of the event, because that is what other people could see and understand. The more the image of God was abstracted from events, the less it communicated. Therefore Israel viewed her history as sacred since it was, in fact, the only way the image of God could be communicated without confusing God with the gods of nature or fertility found in the countries which surrounded the Hebrews.

GOD AND THE IMAGE OF GOD

The image of God that we obtain from studying the Biblical record of revelation is not God. It is an image in the mind and is therefore subject to the limitations that form the mind. The most common illustration would be our own memories of how the image of God has changed in our minds since we were children. As a small child we were unable to reason abstractly, so our knowledge of God was primarily a series of impressions from stories we could understand. Because we lacked general human experience, our notion of God was largely a selfish one rather than including a sense of responsibility for others. Like Paul, when we became adults we put away childish things (1 Corinthians 13:11) and developed a more mature understanding of God. As our awareness and opportunities expanded, so did our image of God enlarge. Our personal history is a long series of adjustments between our experience and our image of God. It is also important to observe that as we mature in our faith, we are constantly modifying our mental image of God; yet we do not look back on our childish notions as wrong— they were right for that stage of development and for the limitation of our mind at that time.

In somewhat the same way we must see the various eras represented in the Bible. As there is development from one era to another, so the image of God changes. Morever, we should expect the image of God to change; since God is God of the living, we have to become aware of his manifestations in each age. When we look at the image of God in some of the oldest periods of the Old Testament, we must not judge these writings on the basis of our present knowledge; we need to understand that the image described is related to the mentality of that period. John Calvin said that God "accommodated" himself to man's condition in these early periods in order that man could know something of God.[4]

The image of God that comes from the Biblical history is not to be communicated as God. The historical images are not to be preserved as complete truth. The actions and moral patterns of behavior that resulted from God's revelation in the particular circumstances of the past are not automatically to become normative for succeeding generations. Why not? Because God is a living will, and this will is to be discerned afresh in each generation amid the changing circumstances of life. God is always related to the present; and because the present is never exactly like the past, the precise meaning of God for us is known only in the present.

Biblical history, then, gives us a picture that we can discern with the mind. It also gives us an indication that God, acting in the present, may be different from the image, since the image is always shaped by the contingencies of past historical episodes. In practical terms, this means that we teach Biblical material in order to transmit a mental picture but we do not want to imply that this mental image is God himself. This is exceedingly difficult to do, but the difference is the difference between being traditional and living a tradition.

An illustration is found in an event in the life of Jesus. The Sadducees, who did not believe in the resurrection, posed an old problem. A man died leaving no children. According to the law of Moses, the man's brother should marry the widow in order to produce children. Each of seven brothers died in turn after marrying the widow, and the Sadducees demanded to know what the marriage situation would be in heaven. Jesus' answer was that they knew "neither the scriptures nor the power of God." In heaven there would be no marriage, and they did not really understand God because "He is not God of the dead, but of the living" (Matthew 22:23-33). This, in short, is the point. If we teach tradition as the substance of faith, we, like the Sadducees, get bogged down, thinking that God is restricted to the past. Rather, we have to see that the image of God comes from the past ("I am the God of Abraham, and the God of Isaac, and the God of Jacob") but the reality of God is in the present.

THE NEW TESTAMENT INTERPRETATION OF THE OLD TESTAMENT

The image of God which we have received from the past must come alive and be related to the present, or it is not an authentic understanding of God. This is an exceedingly difficult idea to communicate even though the Bible itself is a record of God's revelation of his will for particular historical circumstances and is a record of man's increasing—and therefore changing—comprehension of God. Our difficulty in accepting the Bible's interpretation of God is probably rooted in our yearning for security in a hostile world and our desperate search for reassurance against the threat of death. We want the confidence that comes with a recital of God's manifestations in the past. We desire an authentication of past descriptions of God's activity in order to placate the gnawing insecurity in our life. These constant pressures within us tend to make us freeze a conception of the past in a form which fits our present need. Indeed, the very freezing of the past is itself a commentary on our present psychological state. The question posed by the Sadducees is posed all through the Bible and is present in our life: should we freeze the past and then extract the ideas about God from that dead past in order to give us security in the present? The answer our Lord gave to the Sadducees is the answer we find all through the Bible—that God is not the God of the dead but of the living.

Jesus made his affirmation about the living God after he told the Sadducees that they knew neither the Scriptures nor the power of God. This comment about the Scriptures is the key to our problem in the use of the past. We might start our analysis with Jesus himself. We need to remind ourselves that the New Testament is an interpretation of the Old Testament. Christians believe that the New Testament is the fulfillment of the Old; yet the continuation to this day of the Jewish faith is proof enough that the New Covenant as an interpretation of the Old is not shared by all who believe in God's guidance and leadership of Israel.

What, then, was the new revelation that caused the Old Testament to be radically reinterpreted? The answer is Jesus of Nazareth. In Jesus the disciples found a fulfillment of the Old Testament. In him the disciples experienced the Messiah of God. Jesus as a person—who lived, died, and was resurrected and whose Spirit penetrated the disciples as they pondered this new revelation of God in the flesh (Acts 2:1-36)—created the fresh and dynamic interpretation of the Old Testament. This recognition that God had made Jesus both Lord and Christ (Acts 2:36) formed a tradition which developed, and guided the development of, the church. This is the fact of Christianity. It defies rational explanation. It separates Christians from Jews in their religious beliefs. If we do not hold that Jesus of Nazareth is the Christ of God, we cannot claim to be Christian in the New Testament definition and explanation of that term. If we do make that claim, we are saying that God is active in human affairs, revealing his will and guiding an interpretation of his past revelation.

Although it was the resurrection event which formed the Christian tradition and caused a new interpretation of the Old Testament, the disciples were shown how to understand the Old Testament by Jesus himself, as "the climax of the long story of God's dealings with his people."[5] Luke records Jesus' first sermon as based on Isaiah:

> "The Spirit of the Lord is upon me,
> because he has anointed me to preach good news to the poor.
> He has sent me to proclaim release to the captives
> and recovering of sight to the blind,
> to set at liberty those who are oppressed,
> to proclaim the acceptable year of the Lord" (Luke 4:18-19;
> Isaiah 61:1-2).

But rather than discourse on its meaning in verbal form, Jesus said, "Today this scripture has been fulfilled in your hearing" (Luke 4:21). Moreover, Jesus took from Daniel 7 the term "son of man" and applied it to himself. His use of this symbol gathers to his person the hopes of the people of Israel that, in spite of their minority status and defenselessness before the powers of the world, they should have a "kingdom" that "shall not pass away" (Daniel 7:14). In Psalm 118:22-23, we find these words, "The stone which the builders refused is become the head stone of the corner. This is the Lord's doing; it is marvellous in our eyes" (K.J.V.). Mark tells us that Jesus, when opposition developed, identified himself with this stone in a context that shows clearly how he interpreted his role as one sent from God (Mark 12:1-12). The identification that the church made between Jesus and the keystone suggests that the disciples learned the meaning of Jesus from Jesus. When Peter defended himself before Annas, the high priest, he used the same quotation from Psalm 118 to identify Jesus as the indispensable stone in God's building (Acts 4:5-12; see also 1 Peter 2:4-7).

Although Jesus as the fulfillment of the Old Testament expectation concerning a Messiah is the essential element of the New

Testament, we must not overlook Jesus' way of interpreting the religious message of the Old Testament. C.F.D. Moule has pointed out that in Jesus' day there were two major methods of interpretation. The first method "attached a good deal of importance to the traditions of the great rabbis—to traditional interpretations of particular passages handed down communally, by which rules of conduct and other rulings were extracted from the scriptures."[6] The second method was more individualistic. The interpreter, believing God directed the preparation of the words of Scripture, believed also that if he studied the words devotedly, he would understand them directly. In either case, Moule points out, the voice of prophecy was assumed to be silent and authority was sought in the past.

In both of these methods the interpretation of the past was carried out as if the words were themselves inspired rather than the meaning of the words. Words were put together from different parts of the Old Testament on the basis of the surface meaning. For example, the Talmud says, "The dust of the first man was gathered from all over the earth because Ps. 139.16 says God saw the unformed substance, and Zech. 4.10 says the eyes of the Lord run to and fro through the whole earth." Another example is the statement: "That God says his prayers is proved when Isa. 56.7 says *my* (i.e. God's) house of prayer."[7] Jesus, on the contrary, interpreted Scripture on the basis of its inner meaning. The formula found in the Sermon on the Mount is "You have heard that it was said . . . But I say to you . . ." Jesus took the intention of the Mosaic law, and then used that intention in the situation he was facing.

Although the Synoptics contain many examples of Jesus' method of interpretation, the account of his plucking the grain on the Sabbath is typical. The Pharisees asked why he would do this unlawful act. Jesus replied that David, when he was in need of food, entered the Temple and ate bread reserved only for the priests. That human need had priority over ritualistic rules was indicated by Jesus' statement, "The sabbath was made for man, not man for the sabbath" (Mark 2:23-28). On other occasions, Jesus simply quoted the Old Testament without any interpretation, indicating that the message meant what it said. An example of this straightforward use of Scripture is Jesus' reply to the scribe who asked which commandment was first of all. Jesus quoted Deuteronomy 6:4-5: "Hear, O Israel: The Lord our God, the Lord is one; and you shall love the Lord your God with all your heart, and with all your soul, and with all your mind, and with all your strength" (Mark 12:28-31). Thus, the New Testament writer learned from Jesus that he was the fulfillment of the Old Testament and that his method of interpreting the Old Testament was the proper way of understanding God's message from the past. Although there are some illustrations of strained interpretation, allegory, and literalism, in the main the New Testament writers have a fresh and original way of treating the Old Testament.

C. H. Dodd has pointed out that this originality is seen in the material from the Old Testament that was *not* used. There are large sections of the Old Testament relating to a Messiah which were not used by New Testament writers at all. "The whole conception of the Messiah as king, warrior and judge, the ruthless vindicator of the righteousness of God, is absent from the Church's presentation of the Jesus of history . . ."[8] When we examine the writings that were important to Jewish messianic thought, such as Psalms of Solomon, First Enoch, and Fourth Ezra, we find that this material was not used by New Testament writers in relation to Jesus but was used by them to describe Jesus' second coming. Moreover, the Scriptures which the New Testament writers did use to show that Jesus was the Messiah were, for the most part, not considered messianic by Jews of that day. The originality of the New Testament writers is even more pronounced when we realize that the portions of the Old Testament we Christians use today to characterize the Old Testament anticipation of Jesus, such as the suffering servant passage in Isaiah 53, were seldom used by New Testament writers.[9]

The characteristic use of the Old Testament by the New Testament writers is found in Peter's sermon on the Day of Pentecost. There he based his presentation of Jesus as the Messiah on a long quotation from Joel and quoted from Psalms 16, 110, and 132 (Acts 2:14-36). Another tracing of the history of Israel from the standpoint of Jesus was done by Stephen before the high priest

(Acts 7). Paul used the same method in Thessalonica (Acts 17:2-3) and in his defense before Agrippa (Acts 26).[10] Paul's exegesis in Romans 9-11 shows that his method "is to take certain passages of Scripture, to examine them in relation to a broad context, and to determine their meaning and application to the existing situation by comparison with other passages from Scripture."[11] Dodd further points out that Paul's method here is strictly logical and historical; that is, Paul relates the facts of the gospel message to the history of Israel. The same method is used by the writer of Hebrews and also in the more "popular" work, First Peter.

When the full context of the Old Testament material is taken into account, one can see that there is a clearly defined and widely held substructure of belief about the Messiah. Dodd, after classifying the Old Testament material into three major groups, says:

> If we now survey this group of scriptures as a whole, we observe that a single "plot" runs all through. The "hero" suffers shame, ignominy, torment, disaster, and then by sheer grace of God is delivered, raised up, glorified. . . . In Group II, in the main, the suffering and disaster is the judgment of God upon His sinful people, and their restoration is an act of pardon. In Group III, as partly in Group I, the suffering is, in the main, that of an innocent victim, persecuted by the enemies of God. In some measure, however, the two views of suffering are harmonized in the picture of the Suffering Servant in Isa. 52.13—53.12. The sufferings of the Servant are indeed judgment upon sin, but the sin of others, which he bears vicariously. It is thus possible to recognize Christ as the "hero" of the drama of disaster and triumph in all three groups alike. . . . and in His triumph over death and disaster is enacted the promised renovation of the Israel of God, whose sins had brought disaster.[12]

THE OLD TESTAMENT INTERPRETATION OF ITSELF

For the Christian the New Testament is normative. We could probably leave the account of interpretation at this point, but to do so would be to create the false impression that the Old Testament is a continuous line of development which is "real" history rather than interpreted history. Actually, the Old Testament is a story of interpretations of earlier accounts, so that the Old Testament is an illustration both of the nature of revelation and of the way revelation has to be interpreted as it is transmitted from generation to generation. We must recall that the oldest material we have in the Old Testament in its present form are the books of Amos, Hosea, Micah, and Isaiah, written in the eighth century B.C. The Pentateuch and other books related to the formation and development of the nation were put in their present form in the seventh to the fifth century B.C. from oral traditions, written documents, historical records, literary compositions, and songs that reached back to the earliest times. The editors who assembled this material in its present form were influenced by eighth-century prophets; they interpreted the material in line with the theology of the prophets, which emphasized the majesty of God and God's confrontation of man with a challenge to live and act as God's people. The stories of Abraham and the wanderings of the chosen people, of Moses and the settlement of the nation, are all told within the prophetic interpretation of God's covenant with his people.

A specific illustration of how this process of interpretation works out is given by Ernest Wright. In the Old Testament we have two types of covenant. The first type, which is related to Moses, is described in Deuteronomy and Second Kings. It interprets history from the standpoint of great charismatic leaders, appointed by God, and tells how the covenant was broken by people but restored by God. This type of covenant is thought to follow the pattern of political treaties used 2,000 years before Christ.

> The first part of the treaty, composed in the first person, is free narration, never stereotyped, describing the suzerain's benevolent acts to the vassal. Then follow the covenant stipulations, detailing the interests of the suzerain which the vassal vows to observe. The treaty includes the list of witnesses and also the statement of the advantages and disadvantages of obedience ("blessings and curses"), the sanctions in every case being religious. Israel used this type of covenant form to present in objective terms the mutual relation between God and people. Thus obligation was formally set in the context of grace. Indeed this is the only treaty form that permits this rather unique relationship to be expressed in a formal way. Under this analogy, therefore, God appears to Israel as the sovereign of the world who has entered into a special treaty relation with one people, though at the same time his royal relation to all peoples is affirmed.[13]

The second type of covenant is related to David, and is described in First and Second Chronicles, Ezra and Nehemiah. These accounts were written after the Exile, when the Hebrews were struggling to regain their national identity and self-respect. This type of political treaty is a special type in which "the divine council members selected and empowered the king and committed themselves to support him in the office. In Israel this treaty form found expression in God's covenant with David, wherein God committed himself to sustain the dynasty."[14] This covenant, like the Mosaic one, showed God's love for his people, but this second one functions through the king as God's representative.

Each of these two main streams of interpretation of the history of Israel used a different type of treaty as a model for a conception of the covenant. After the Exile, the Davidic covenant was emphasized because it was believed that part of the nation's difficulties were due to its inability to keep the Mosaic covenant. The mass of laws that had developed in the Mosaic tradition were codified and made a "constitution" for the nation and put in the form in which they now appear in Deuteronomy.

People of every age represented in the Bible interpreted the history of the past in the light of the circumstances they faced. The situation after the Exile, just referred to, required that Israel develop an understanding of her past to account for the captivity of the nation and to provide hope for the future; and she did this by her interpretation of her past through the mind of the great prophets. We see this same phenomenon in Jesus' day. Palestine was an occupied country. Although Rome allowed a certain amount of self-rule, the real political authority was exercised by Roman governors. Again the question was, "Why is Israel in such an ignoble condition and what must we do to regain God's favor and our own national integrity?" The Pharisees answered this question by saying that the nation had neglected God's laws; if the people would but dedicate themselves to the careful obedience to the law of Moses, God would intervene and re-establish his kingdom. The Zealots, on the other hand, believed that Israel would never recapture her glory unless she used military means to overthrow the Romans; and they interpreted Israel's history to justify that position. The Sadducees represented those who believed that they should accept the present political condition and make the most of their limited freedom; being in control of the Temple, they were in a position to negotiate with Rome. They also tended to modify some of the teachings, such as the resurrection of the dead, probably because they were secularized in theology as well as politics. The Essenes were in opposition to all of these parties. They believed that it was only in purity of life, disassociated from the compromises and ambiguities of the world, that the soul of Israel could be saved; so they withdrew from society and lived simple, monastic lives in caves.

Jesus' life and teachings, seen in the context of these four schools of interpretation, show the startling nature of his interpretation of himself as the Messiah, of his method of going back to God's intention in the law and to God's revelation in Israel's history, and then of recasting that intention in the conditions he found in Palestine. This method caused his audience to be "astonished at his teaching, for he taught them as one who had authority, and not as their scribes" (Matthew 7:28-29).

BIBLICAL INTERPRETATION TODAY

Let us pause to review the discussion thus far. New Testament writers, we have said, interpreted Jesus' life as the fulfillment of the Old Testament prophecy. Christians believe that Jesus is the incarnation of God and do not expect any further revelation of this nature except the final coming of Christ. Salvation depends on faith in him, and no contemporary interpretation of Jesus is expected to change the centrality of Jesus for Christians.

We have also said that Jesus demonstrated to the disciples a method of interpretation whereby Old Testament passages were selected to show the full counsel of God for his people, rather than a literal word-for-word type of interpretation. This truly historical way of interpreting the past was also used by the leading writers of Israel after the Exile and in other periods of Biblical record. The reason we have to interpret past revelation is because of the nature of revelation. Revelation in the Bible is particular— that is, it occurs in specific human conditions that are culturally defined. Strictly speaking, the revelation is for the special set of circumstances. It is this particularity of revelation that gives it its power. The persons involved are confident of God's preservation and direction in the reality they face. Although they do not know precisely how their actions will evolve, they are confident that they speak the proper word for God and do the right thing for his cause. Revelation is present rather than future; so, in succeeding generations, the revelatory experience has to be reinterpreted to be useful. Perhaps a more accurate way of stating the matter would be to say that Biblical revelation occurs in an ongoing stream of God's people and the conceptualization of revelation is only a way to remember the experience. For the past to be significant it must be interpreted. The genius of the Hebrews was their ability to go back to accounts of God's past revelation and reinterpret them in the light of new conditions which developed in their history. The past must become contemporary before it can become significant.

We must be clear that this process of interpretation is different from extracting general principles from the past and applying them to the present. Since God is the source of revelation in the past and present, we cannot conceive of the task as application. Rather, we have to see that as God's will fitted certain conditions of the past, so his will is to be discerned in present concrete conditions. Because God's will is a part of his sovereignty and because conditions today are never like the past, we have to read the present through the past.

The process of interpretation also requires that present believers be active in trying to understand and do God's will in the present; therefore, it is not sufficient to make the transmissive process exclusively mental. The process is first mental, but in the end it has to be situational. An analogy with politics may be helpful. We can learn about politics from books, but we do not understand politics nor do we achieve anything politically until we attempt to be political. Then we learn that although books give us a correct description of politics, politicians are human; there are scores of factors, contingencies, and uncertainties in a specific situation which are not amenable to rational control—only judgment built on general experience in dealing with people will be useful. So to move from the mental grasp of meaning to any concrete human situation requires that we take seriously the particular configuration of factors which characterizes a human problem.

The crucial matter therefore is transmission. Theology cannot be complete until it is practical theology; that is, until the historical tradition has interacted with the living, human situation. According to our Biblical model of interpretation, past historical revelations of God must be interpreted under the leadings of God's Spirit, who will guide us to truth (John 14:25-26; 16:12-15). This characteristic of God, that he is known as we attempt to live our interpretation of past revelation, seems to make our knowledge of God completely subjective and under the control of current events. Such is not the case. Rather, we have been saying that we can understand the past only as we situationalize it.

PERENNIAL HUMAN SITUATIONS

So far, we have been discussing the unique and central historical experiences which form the Biblical revelation of God. For these parts of the Bible we have to develop a method of historical interpretation in order to appropriate meaning for today. Now we must recognize that the Bible also contains a vast amount of nonhistorical material which deals with perennial human situations. Although the material has some of the outward character of history and did evolve in a historical setting, the substance deals with human conditions which transcend time and culture.

This type of material is sprinkled all through the Bible. The larger sections are found in the Psalms, Job, Proverbs, the parables of Jesus, and the apocalyptic books. We could suggest that this material be interpreted piece by piece to form and guide our experiences. This method has the advantage of treating the material for what it is in its literary form—whether a song, poem, vision, or parable; also, it honors the historical context that may have shaped the message. But this method has the disadvantage of starting with teachings for which a person may not be ready, and the message therefore may not be adequately communicated.

Probably a better method of using the nonhistorical material would be to relate it to life situations as they emerge. When Jesus was confronted with a specific human situation he would often quote Scripture that was applicable to the conditions at hand. The temptations were remembered by the church as each concluding with a Scripture passage which both explained Jesus' refusal to be tempted and affirmed his loyalty to God's purposes (Matthew 4:1-11). When Jesus was asked to summarize the law, he did so with a direct quotation of the Shema from Deuteronomy 6:4-5 and Leviticus 19:18 (see Mark 12:28-34). When asked about divorce, Jesus quoted directly from Deuteronomy 24:1-4 and elaborated the ideal of marriage as a lifelong relationship (see Mark 10:2-9). With very few exceptions the Synoptic Gospels show that when Jesus was faced with one of the perennial human conditions, he used Old Testament quotations to make an affirmation about God's teaching on the matter, as if there were little difference between past teachings and the present.

The New Testament church followed Jesus' example in their use of the teachings of Jesus. The bulk of this new material was in parables. We now have evidence to support the idea that these teachings go back more closely to the historical Jesus than anything else in the New Testament. These parables were collected soon after Jesus' death and were in circulation for instructional purposes. Unfortunately, the setting in which many of the parables were spoken was not recorded; so the Gospel writers fitted some of them into different settings.[15] It is this lack of interest in the actual setting in which the parable was originally spoken which indicates that the newly formed churches used some of them as timeless truths. We would concur with their judgment, because some parables give us a clear idea of what it means to live a Christian life. The remarkable power of the parables to stand thousands of years and to transcend various cultures so that they speak directly to us today is related to the perennial nature of the human experience about which they were used. We can recognize the prodigal son (Luke 15:11-32) in our neighborhood and the good Samaritan (Luke 10:29-37) on almost any modern highway; and the unjust steward (Luke 16:1-9) appears with almost monotonous regularity in our political and business organizations.

The form in which the perennial human conditions emerge may vary in different historical periods, but the underlying reality is the same. For these perennial conditions there is no solution or answer—there is only the affirmation that comes from one's belief. These human conditions are described in many religions of the world and constitute the area of our life where decisions have to be made almost every day. There is no way to be objective about these matters; one's emotions are deeply involved. The Christian faith has its own definition and affirmation about these human conditions, and these are carried in the living community of believers from one generation to another.

As a person experiences one of these human situations, he is led back to the Biblical material for the faith-affirmation that shapes his response to the condition he experiences. Bible study helps to define the nature of these human conditions, to sharpen one's perception of them in the ordinary round of living, and to anticipate the outcome of them in subsequent human actions. This latter observation is particularly true of personal moral actions, for the Bible is full of case studies of how one immoral action produces consequences that go on to "the third and fourth generation."

Comparison of past and present is possible because the human reality is the same. The function of practical theology is to clear away the cultural obstructions and social accretions that would hinder a person from seeing the connection between himself and the experiences of others. Our interpretive rule might be worded thus: the extent to which the past human condition is like our condition is the extent to which we can incorporate the Biblical teaching as our own. For many of the personal human conditions, such as sexual morality, we have little trouble showing that the present conditions are not unlike those of the Bible, except in minor detail. On the other hand, atomic war is different from past wars in that the thermonuclear explosion poisons the air and the ground so that we punish future generations. The causes of war seem to remain somewhat the same, but the techniques that we have developed bring about a new condition which makes past affirmations about war unreliable for our present nuclear age.

What, then, are the perennial human conditions to which the Christian religion gives a faith-affirmation?

Evil.   The book of Job is a classic effort to probe the meaning of the presence of evil in the world. In Job we find a description of how unexpectedly tragedy strikes. Job refuses to accept the theology of the day that evil is the result of sin and wealth is the result of goodness. His theology is expressed in the words, "Shall we receive good at the hand of God, and shall we not receive evil?" (Job 2:10). Although Job searches diligently for a solution, no solution is given except the resolute effort to be faithful to God (Job 13:15). Jesus confirms our inability to penetrate the reason for evil in the world by his parable of the Wheat and the Weeds, saying that good and evil will always be intermingled until the end of the world (Matthew 13:24-30). Although God is love and God is good, he permits evil to operate in the world and we have no assurance that it will ever be different. We have only the affirmation that in Jesus Christ we will have power to "overcome evil with good" (Romans 12:21).

Death. Probably life is more of a mystery than death. We self-conscious creatures cannot understand the origin of life or the purpose of life any better than those who told the stories in the first chapters of Genesis. Moreover, our much praised control of nature, our recent probing of the smallest particles that make up matter, and our discoveries in space have given us no answer— only more mystery. The more we know, the more tragic death becomes; yet death is the end of all living things. When a person faces his own death rather than death as a general condition, he has to make some kind of reconciliation with life. When we face our death, we face the same mystery we found when we came into a conscious awareness of life, for which there is no logical explanation. We Christians have the faith-affirmation that God created the world for his glory and that in his wisdom death is a part of the process. We have the faith-affirmation that "the wages of sin is death, but the free gift of God is eternal life in Christ Jesus our Lord" (Romans 6:23).

Sin. From the story of Adam and Eve onward, the Bible is one continuous commentary on sin. There is hardly a chapter in the Bible that does not refer to sin in some form. The history of Israel is a recital of the nation's failure to live up to a covenant promise made at Sinai. Individual accounts of sin such as David's desire for

Bathsheba (2 Samuel 11-12) or Ananias and Sapphira's greed (Acts 5:1-11) are told in enough detail for us not only to understand the case but also to identify the same temptations in our own life. However, in the Biblical accounts of sin we usually find the offer of God's grace. There is condemnation of sin in the sinner, but there is also an offer on God's part to heal the wounds of sin. The death of Jesus was interpreted by the church as atonement for sin. The oldest tradition of the disciples is the good news that God had visited and redeemed his people. The kerygma, which is the heart of the earliest preachings we have recorded in the New Testament, is a constant reiteration of Christ's dying for our sins; this is exemplified by Paul in 1 Corinthians, chapter 15, where he states the tradition as it came to him, "that Christ died for our sins in accordance with the scriptures . . ." Today, two thousand years after those words were written, we have nothing new to add to that faith-affirmation that Christ is the lamb of God that takes away the sins of the world, although we may need to state it in a fresh way (see 1 John 1:8-9).

Personal Ethics.   Next to sin, there is no human condition that is treated more often in the Bible than morality. The earliest accounts that we have of man in the Bible show him struggling with an answer to the question, "Am I my brother's keeper?" The problem of the "oughtness" in human relations is perennial. The Ten Commandments, for example, have stood for thousands of years as a summary of moral standards that must characterize our interpersonal relations in order to have an enduring society. The wisdom literature of the Old Testament, especially the Proverbs, consists of wise folk sayings that were hammered out over hundreds of years to guide people in a multitude of everyday relationships. The Sermon on the Mount, the parables, the ethical instructions of the early church as found in Paul's writings, all pound away at human conditions to which the Christian must make a moral response.

There may be a sense in which we could argue for moral standards and moral actions based on purely human considerations and say that prohibition against murder is found in many societies untouched by Biblical influence. The motive power for such a system of morals is enlightened self-interest. The Bible, to the contrary, takes the position that morality is a result of the believer's relationship to God, that one lives a moral life because this is something he can offer to God in gratitude for what God has done for him. The Ten Commandments should not be read by themselves but should always be read in the context of the covenant ceremony in Exodus, chapter 19. Then the great faith-affirmation, "I am the LORD your God, who brought you out of the land of Egypt, out of the house of bondage" (Exodus 20:2), sets the stage for the moral behavior of God's chosen people.

Since our concern here is the use of Biblical material rather than a cataloguing of the teachings of the Bible in relation to the many kinds of moral problems men encounter, we must observe that some discrimination must be exercised concerning what constitutes a perennial human moral problem. Homosexuality is condemned without reservation by Paul and presumably by the early church (1 Corinthians 6:9-10). Today we would disapprove of homosexuality, but we tend to treat it as a psychiatric or physiological disorder and enlist medical aid for the treatment of such persons. Sexual desire, however, has not changed. The differences between David's lack of moral sensitivity in his relationship to Bathsheba and to her husband Uriah is different only in detail from the action of many contemporary leaders. Although society today has rules of divorce and provision for the physical care of children from broken homes, the basic human condition of sexual desire which motivates some divorces has not changed since the writing of the Ten Commandments. This same observation might be made of honesty. Although the precise definition of what constitutes honesty is different today from that of previous eras, the causes of dishonesty—such as desire for wealth or the attempt to enhance one's reputation—remain the same. Also, we have to separate for moral consideration those matters of custom that change from age to age. Paul's instruction that women should not speak in the church (1 Corinthians 14:34) is widely rejected today as inconsistent with our understanding of human nature and with Paul's own comment that in Christ there is "neither male nor female" (Galatians 3:28).

In this area of perennial human conditions, therefore, we must first use our critical intelligence to separate the matters of custom from those of genuine moral concern. Next, we must study the human problems to see if we have new understanding which would cause us to modify the Biblical affirmations (as in regard to homosexuality). Then we are prepared to strip down the contemporary situation or the Biblical story to its basic human condition, to identify the matter to which we bring our faith-affirmation. The hinge by which we swing from past to present is the human situation. Whether we start with the Bible or with the contemporary situation is not significant in itself so long as we go through this process of bringing faith-affirmation to bear on perennial human conditions.

In developing a way to approach Biblical interpretation, not all of the possible human conditions that transcend time and to which we can make faith-affirmations need be mentioned. A more complete consideration would include vocation, the way man uses his life. Although the social order has changed unbelievably, man in a modern industrial technical civilization still has the choice of using his life in different ways, and the values that underlie his choice are not different from those of the past. Stewardship should also absorb our attention. Man from the earliest time was told to "be fruitful and multiply, and fill the earth and subdue it . . ." (Genesis 1:28). We have learned many ways to use the treasures of the earth, but the problem of a judicial use of, and a fair distribution of, the world's natural resources plagues us as completely today as it did in Abraham's time.

BELIEFS AND VALUES

This chapter has not attempted to work out a set of values that are offered as the substance of the Christian faith. To do so would violate the nature of this approach to communication. In order for a community of believers to communicate a faith that is more Christian than that which they are already communicating, they must learn to interpret the Bible historically, which requires that they open themselves to the leading of God's Spirit. They must analyze the human situation they face in relation to similar situations in the Bible in order to judge whether the Biblical affirmations apply to the contemporary situation or whether they must develop new values. Since religious beliefs function as values, we must constantly state, test, and reformulate our beliefs.

This process may seem so complex and demanding to the average congregation that they will say it is impossible. To such an objection we would repeat what has been said in several places in this book. The process of socialization goes on, and all adults are involved in it. The only issue before us is whether we will become more conscious of our own part in the process and more concerned to find "the mind of Christ" (Philippians 2:1-11). If we are, then we will "grow in . . . grace and knowledge" (2 Peter 3:18) and our growth will communicate faith because we are in touch with the Source of faith.

VII

Guidelines for Communicating Faith

As indicated in the first chapter, there is no obvious, utilitarian connection between a theory of communication and the practical problems in the church. Matters such as the size of a church school class or the use of mechanical aids in teaching may be related to a theory of communication; but in actual practice almost all theories use the same methods. The way in which a method or a mechanical aid is used may be influenced by your theory of communication. Preaching is a good illustration. Religious groups of all types in the whole spectrum of the Judeo-Christian tradition use preaching; but the way it is used by the Quakers is different from the use made by Presbyterians, by leaders of a revivalist sect, or by the Roman Catholic Church. A theory helps us set goals for our work, suggests a starting place, gives us a basis for allocating our time and money to various means of communication, and provides a basis for judging our effectiveness. In short, a theory should help us find guidelines for our work.

Throughout this book I have used the general term "community of believers" in order to focus attention on the communal nature of the Christian faith and to avoid any hard-and-fast identification with the institutionalized church. God's Spirit has on many occasions broken out of established institutional structures to form new communities and new ways of worship and service, and we must assume that this may be happening now. However, the local congregation has been a characteristic form of the church since New Testament times; therefore, in this brief discussion of a model I shall have in mind a local congregation.

THE CENTRALITY OF THE CONGREGATION

Our major mistake in Protestantism has been the assumption—made especially acute by the rise of the religious education movement at the beginning of the twentieth century—that the communication of faith was, in the greater part, directly dependent upon classroom instruction of children and youth. This is not the place to analyze that situation in detail, but we are now aware that Protestants are in a state of crisis in relation to educational strategy. In brief, our present strategy was formed during the period when a Protestant ethos characterized our nation. Under such circumstances, the Sunday school and other part-time voluntary agencies of instruction were satisfactory. Now, in an era of radical pluralism in which we have a wide variety of religious groups and a large secular or humanist group, we Protestants find that the basic strategy developed over a century ago is inadequate for the cultural situation in which we live.[1]

The first thing we have to do in this approach is to remove from our minds the notion that the communication of the Christian faith is directly dependent upon any instructional agencies or methods and fix in our minds the idea that faith is fostered by a community of believers, usually a congregation. Instruction is a necessary part of the life of the congregation, but instruction must be related to the life of the congregation. Along with this shift of focus from the instructional agencies of the congregation to the congregation itself, we must abandon our cherished American individualism. Education—especially that of children—is always focused on the individual; yet this can be done without making the individual the center of the educational process. We can excuse the nineteenth-century Protestant for his individualism because of the frontier situation in that era and because the social sciences had not yet developed an understanding of the process of socialization. Today, we must return to the Biblical view that a person is the product of his culturing group.[2]

We start then with the congregation as the primary society of Christians and say that life together is the method and the quality of what is communicated. This is a description of a *process*, and it is important to separate this process from what we think ought to be communicated; but until we get this *process* in mind we cannot make much use of this approach. A sleepy rural church that grinds through a traditional program teaches that Christianity is a set of beliefs and customs. A small remnant of white Protestants in a large, ornate imitation Gothic building located in what was once a fashionable neighborhood but is now called an "inner-city situation" is demonstrating its beliefs when it maintains a clublike gathering of people with similar backgrounds and personal interests. Contrariwise, a congregation that is seriously searching for God's leading, made up of individuals who are consciously coaching each other on ways they can actualize their ministry for Christ in their community, communicates their yearning as well as their interpretation of Christianity.

This proposition seems so simple to me that I feel embarrassed to record it. However, on many occasions when I have voiced this idea to ministers, most will agree; but after a while one will say, "You know the trouble in my church is the Sunday school, and I must do something about it. Where can I get a better curriculum?" I usually reply, "Do you mean a *printed* curriculum?" Then after waiting a few minutes until the meaning of my question has become clear, I continue, "What would be different in your church if you ordered your printed instructional materials from a different address?" This question does not solve the problem. Yet, it forces the questioner to see that the human community is the place where one must start and that printed curriculum materials can support but can seldom create change.

After seeing that the group of believers is the unit with which we must work, we must then see that whatever is done or said, or not done or not said, *is* teaching. There is no such thing as postponing the solution to a problem. The decision to postpone is a decision; it teaches that the issue is too hot to handle, that such issues are not appropriate for the church, or that the tactic of postponement is more important at this point than a resolution to settle the matter. People learn from the way events are handled. There is no neutrality. If a congregation attempts to be neutral, it teaches that on the issues at hand it can't make up its mind, it is fearful of the result of a decision, or it is confused about how to proceed. There is no avoidance of an issue. Not to see an issue is to teach that Christians do not see issues. Christians who avoid problems in social ethics—such as involvement in racial relations, war, or the distribution of wealth—are saying that the Christian faith does not operate in these areas. We must see the congregation as a field of forces—individuals and groups—in lively interaction with each other; the grist of this interactional process *is* the content of their faith. We must see the congregation as a force in a field of other forces in the community. What the congregation as a group says and does in the community is the meaning they give to their faith. If we practice our theology within this interactive frame of reference, we will then be able to see that the functions of worship, searching (study), development of ethical positions on issues, and ministry to the community are all subordinate to the congregation's purpose of being the people of God in a certain time and place.

INTERPRETATION—THE DOMINANT ACTIVITY

In order to be the people of God, the congregation must see itself as living in a stream of interpreted history. This approach keeps us from falling into the commonly held notion that the Christian faith is an absolute which we discover with the help of our theology and then apply to situations we face. Christianity in this latter sense is an abstraction, and our efforts to apply it usually take the form of saying what we think should be done without any serious consideration of whether it actually can be done. Rather, we must see ourselves as interpreting a tradition that was in its day an interpretation. The reality with which we must work is the community of believers; in order to gain perspective on ourselves we need constantly to go back to the experiences which other generations have had with God in order to understand how God works through his church and through the world of human events. We cannot get a perspective without comparison. We cannot know God except as we know how other generations responded to him.

To identify the congregation's dominant activity as interpretation forces us to focus attention on the interactional process as well as on the tradition we have received. We have to see that the unique aspect of our relation with each other is our faith, regardless of how weak or immature it may be; that we learn to receive the gift of grace as we practice it in relation to each other; that the ties of affection we have with each other are the only foundation which will support our differences of opinion; and that as a group we have to search for the meaning of our faith in the past and then test it in the present. This process is a long way from the method of applying intellectual formulation to specific problems.

The congregation, then, is a school of faith. All that the congregation does is both a means of communicating the faith and a subject of investigation. This must not be taken to the extreme by the congregations so that they become "paralyzed by analysis," but this is not likely to happen in America. The opposite is most likely the case—the congregation becoming tradition-bound. It is that condition we must fight.

How can we avoid being tradition-bound yet honor our tradition? We must subject our activities to systematic study and make appropriate changes. Worship, for example, is something that we do every Sunday according to a traditional pattern; yet seldom does a congregation know why we have the pattern, much less that it might be changed. Every aspect of worship could be the subject of investigation. At the end of a year or two, some new forms might be developed and new ways of congregational participation be evolved, or else the old ones might be retained because they are better understood. The sacraments are seldom explained except to the confirmation classes, yet we use them constantly. It is important for adults, who often have only a vague idea of what the Lord's Supper means or who have lost their sense of the meaning of the ritual, to have a chance to look afresh at the way this sacrament came into being. In some areas it would be a shock to Christians to learn that Jesus used wine and not Welch's grape juice. From that trivial fact they could start to learn how their own American pietistic tradition had interpreted the Bible; thus, in small ways they might begin to develop a historical perspective which should mature so that they could become able to transpose the meaning of other events from the first to the twentieth century.

These standard elements of worship are a good illustration of the problems we face. Normally, the child at confirmation receives a theologically correct definition of the traditional belief about worship and sacraments, and there the matter lies for the rest of his life. Unless the child is unusually inquisitive, he gets no further instruction except what may come incidentally in communion sermons. His mind is religiously arrested at the teen-age level. But the child grows, his mind expands, experiences that were anticipated (such as vocation, marriage, parenthood) become personal to him; yet, his understanding of the Christian faith remains where it was when he was a young teen-ager. The congregation needs to continue to interpret its worship and sacraments to the growing person on through the life cycle, deepening and enriching their meaning as the person becomes more capable of responding to the depths of understanding which are conveyed by the symbols in the sacrament.

Along with this need for the congregation to continually interpret its worship to members at various maturity levels, the congregation needs to interpret the nature and the ministry of the church to its members, especially to new members. The way in which the normal Protestant church receives adult members is a reliable guide to what that church is. Too often the process is casual: no more is demanded of the prospective member than that he show an interest in religion or certify that in the past he belonged to a congregation somewhere. Whatever meaning the Christian faith has must be made manifest as a part of the act of joining. There are few times in the life of a person when education can be as effective as at the time of joining a church. Let me repeat the saying of Kurt Lewin, "Learning is first a new belonging." The congregation must maintain a comprehensive, educational plan for receiving new members. This would include vigorous study for at least three months, the act of joining, and a continuation of training for at least three more months so that the individual may find ways to minister in the name of Christ. This latter segment of membership training is almost totally absent from Protestant church life today. If the congregation is the community of believers, then we must make the act of joining an integral part of the process of "belonging." It is *after* a person has made a decision that he is psychologically most open to an explanation of the fullest meaning of his decision. If the decision has any significance at all, he tests that decision in his daily round of activities to see what difference that new belonging makes.[3]

We must move into this natural, psychological state and help the new member find his ministry, or else we teach (remember there is no neutrality!) that membership consists of just "going to church." We cannot honestly say to church members that they should have a ministry unless we help them find such a ministry. The problem is as old as 1 Corinthians 12-13. We would agree with Paul that people have a variety of gifts, and that they should find the way they can use their gifts for the upbuilding of the body of Christ while they also find and practice the more "excellent way" of love in human relations. But we must define "belonging" so that a person makes a conscious decision about what he will do with his personal gifts in a particular ministry. We should be as practical and concrete about this aspect of belonging as we are about explaining the budget and handing the new member a pledge card to sign!

The budget of the congregation is a theological statement of belief. The budget may have more power to convey the real beliefs of the congregation than the educational program, and we should spend more time developing the budget so that a wide representation of the members can participate in its planning. The standard items all need more attention. Is the percentage of the budget for creature comforts for the congregation out of line with what is used in a ministry to the community? To state the question that way raises the question of the role of the church in the community. Should the church pay taxes for what it receives from the community? If not taxes, should the church pay a token amount in lieu of taxes to demonstrate that it wants to help carry the cost of education, police, fire protection? Should the church set up a child guidance clinic, or use its facilities for tutoring student dropouts? Questions of the church's proper function come alive in the budget preparation, and such questions should be encouraged and made the subject of investigations. We should raise questions such as these: Is this proposed expenditure appropriate to the ministry in

Christ which we as a church are attempting in this community? Is our congregation the proper one to do this, or should we co-ordinate our work with some other agency or churches? To ask these and related questions is to open up an awareness of what the congregation may do to be an extension of Christ's ministry in the world. *Not* to ask this type of question is to reinforce the notion that the budget is only an organized way to pay running expenses and that the church has little interest in events taking place around it.[4]

The buildings and physical surroundings of the congregation provide more data about the beliefs which really function within the life of the congregation. Buildings are solidified ideas. If the congregation has attempted to build a cathedral—allocating its attention to all of the details necessary to erect and maintain this type of edifice—it must in all honesty label the building a museum or a pride symbol. Sunday school lessons on humility have little meaning in a congregation that is spending most of its time and money on a building as a status symbol: what is learned under such circumstances is that a person should appear to be modest while he struggles to impress other people. The physical location and the character of the church property all say something about the beliefs of the congregation. Perhaps we should rethink the whole matter of holding property, for most of our waste is at this point. We have billions of dollars invested in buildings that are seldom used. A congregation ought to consider whether its living of the faith cannot be done more appropriately in rented buildings, in buildings shared with congregations of other faiths, or in commercial buildings that are idle on weekends. The churches of America could preach an unforgettable sermon by cashing in much of their property, moving to less pretentious quarters, and using that money in their ministry.

We could go on and discuss the administrative policies of the congregation or the salary schedule of employees as illustrating how the local congregation in its life lives an interpretation of the tradition it proclaims, but additional areas for examination are not necessary. It may be necessary to say again that this interpretation by the congregation of its functions is not something we add, nor is it a program to be superimposed on activities already going on; it is a normal and necessary part of the congregational life. The only issues before us are whether we will be aware of the process of communication that is going on by reason of the choices our congregation makes and whether we will deliberately use these choices to reflect the meaning of our faith.

THE SHAPING OF MENTALITY

We started with the most obvious and visible aspects of congregational life to illustrate the inevitability of the congregation's interpreting the meaning of faith in relation to its life as an institution in the community. Now we must look closely at the more deliberate efforts of the Christian community to form the mentality of its members: preaching and teaching.

Since this is not an essay on homiletics, the sermon as such will not be discussed except to say that it is one of the principal means of interpreting the contemporary meaning of the Christian faith and therefore the shaping of the mentality of Christians. In the average Protestant church the minister is the only trained interpreter of tradition, and he is the principal leader of the congregation's life. Sermons reach more of the adults of the congregation than any other efforts to interpret the Christian message, so we start with them.

Different religious traditions interpret the role of the sermon differently. These interpretations range from that of the Quakers, who have no formal sermon, to that of the Presbyterians and Lutherans, who often insist that the sermon is the contemporary word of God. All traditions that use the sermon consider it to be contemporary speech about God in the light of the past, regardless of how effective it is expected to be for the present. My personal feeling is that the sermon can be a useful way to mold Christian mentality but that it can be more effective if it is considered a part of the ongoing life of the congregation than if it is a feature of the worship or the principal activity of the minister. To consider the sermon a part of the ongoing life of the congregation would require a basic reformulation of the method by which sermons are planned and used.

The normal method is for the minister to preach on whatever topics seem right to him. He may use topics appropriate to the liturgical year, special events in the community, or problems that arise in the congregation. Once preached, the sermon has completed its usefulness except for occasional mimeographing for wider distribution. I believe we must maintain the autonomy of the pulpit and must create a climate of opinion which will support the right of the minister to preach on whatever topic seems appropriate to him. Freedom of the pulpit—like academic freedom in the university—will be abused, but in the long run it is the only way for a prophetic voice to be heard. A minister should approach his preaching with the reverence that is appropriate for such an important task. Whatever weaknesses he may have in preparation and training, he is responsible to God for whatever he says. It is for this reason that I do not believe it is appropriate to have a discussion of the sermon soon after its delivery; this plan sets up a situation where the minister becomes too conscious of his auditors, nor does it give them enough time to brood over the sermon.

A better plan would be to see the sermon as the minister's unique part in a variety of interpreted actions participated in by the congregation during the week. When he was a minister in a church in the East Harlem Protestant Parish, George W. Webber developed a lectionary of Biblical passages to be used through the week by all of the groups in the church. On Wednesday nights, adults and church school teachers in home meetings went over the passage with commentaries to find its meaning for their situation, and on Sunday that passage was the Biblical reference for the sermon. Other groups meeting at other times, including the church school, also used the selected passage for the week. The congregation by searching the Scripture in a variety of ways had some sense of unity as God's people and of mutual interdependence in finding God's word of guidance for themselves. This or some similar arrangement makes the shaping of a Christian mentality the first order of business for the whole congregation rather than just for the educational specialists or the ordained clergy; yet the sermon and the church school class each has its distinct place.[5]

The sermon can be built into the ongoing life of the congregation in other ways. A youth group or adult group could request a series of sermons on a particular subject and ask for copies for discussion purposes. If the minister is not present for the discussion, the group should summarize their reactions to the sermon and send them to him.

Today there is no liturgical reason why laymen should not participate in the worship, leading various parts or composing prayers. The minister might for symbolic purpose come down into the congregation for pastoral prayers or ask for various concerns that should be incorporated in the pastoral prayers. The announcement period does not have to be a recital of information already mimeographed in the church bulletin and held in everyone's hands. The announcements could consist of brief comments about the program or problems the church is having in its various ministries. It could be important to hear a news report from some church group, a recounting of an insight into a Biblical passage which has appeared spontaneously in a class, or an enumeration of the docket faced by the official board with a request for prayers for guidance, a short account of an event involving the way some church met a difficult problem creatively, or an excerpt from a soldier's letter describing what he was up against on the battlefield, and so on. There are many ways a congregation can keep itself informed about its ongoing life rather than concentrating on organizational machinery.[6]

DEVELOPING CRITICAL INTELLIGENCE

Part of the shaping of Christian mentality is the development of critical intelligence. Although all aspects of congregational life contribute to the shaping, the role is normally played by organized study groups.[7] This approach to communication would insist that our strategy in formal, educational work start with, and be centered in, the communicant members of the church. This is so because adults are the people responsible for the decisions which make the congregation what it is, they are the influential agencies in the home and society, and they are the only ones with enough maturity to evaluate the tradition critically. Such an approach is different from the strategy formed in the early nineteenth century by evangelical theology which assumed that the Sunday school was a preparation for conversion or for membership in the church. This approach is different from the strategy formed in the early twentieth century by the liberal religious educator who, with his new psychological understanding of the child, wanted to make personal experience the center of the religious education process.[8] Both of these strategies were child-centered and highly individualistic.

This approach—the congregation as the primary society and faith in God as the goal—requires adult believers to be the agents of communication in all relationships and assumes that the range of awareness and quality of life cannot go much beyond where the adults are in their spiritual discernment.[9] While the strategy centers on adults, its purpose is to help adults live, test, and modify the Christian tradition to fit situations they are facing. Enough has been said in previous chapters about the kind of interpretation that must go on in order to live the tradition, so we shall simply indicate here a variety of practical ways this can be done in a Protestant congregation.

We should face realistically the major problem involved in any effort to train the laity of a congregation. Adults are not like children. They already have acquired the basic patterns of thought, action, and skills necessary to carry on their life. They do not readily see the need for any organized serious study of religion. They may see the need for study related to their profession, for such study helps them advance in their work. But their religious development too often has been arrested back in childhood. Because their deep and often unconscious emotions are related to the attitudes their parents had and the way their parents implanted a conscience within them, they cannot easily open this area of their life to the rational processes of the mind. That is why adults are so defensive or aggressive in the church when some idea or proposal runs counter to the older and deeper emotionalized attitudes that occupy the substructure of their personality. Also, many adults had unfortunate experiences with classroom instruction in their childhood. They were caught in a competitive situation where they could not excel, they were graded unfairly, or most likely they saw little connection between organized study and the human problems they had to solve. The average adult is a battle-scarred veteran in classroom instruction, so he is wary of additional group study.[10]

It is also true that some of the adults in a church will have had good experiences in classroom instruction in the past and will be eager to continue to grow in their understanding of religion. The rapid expansion of departments of religion in state and independent universities and the large enrollment in these classes indicate a seriousness about religion and a desire to explore religious questions. This generation of young people will be in our churches in a few years to enrich the number of young adults who have had a taste of what education in religion can be. We must provide opportunity for these people to continue to probe the meaning of religion and must use them as yeast to permeate the body of conventional Christians who are apprehensive about serious study.

These comments are made to dispel any notion that, if we just reverse the strategy of the Sunday school and of the liberal religious education movement and focus attention on adults rather than on children, we automatically will solve our problem of communicating faith. We will indeed have a strategy which will allow the natural socialization process to work effectively, but we cannot assume that adults will respond to the same educational efforts we have learned to use for children and youth. Although there is an accumulated body of material about how adults learn when they are motivated by economic necessity, we do not have a clear understanding of how adults learn in informal, voluntary associations such as the church; nor do we have dependable knowledge of how adults change their values and world view except as it is done in relation to the primary societies to which they give allegiance. So we are in a situation which requires that we change our basic strategy, but we are not able to offer assurance that any particular program of adult education will be satisfactory.

We must therefore reassure ourselves that the congregational approach is, in spite of all its difficulties, the one that makes progress—even though it is the advance of the turtle rather than of the jack rabbit. Once we have made that determination, then we can see all the natural structures of the congregation as possibilities for enlightenment, expansion of awareness, and education. We will have great flexibility in our approach to education if we make short-range plans and if we are able to try many different ways of education—depending on the situation in the congregation, the age, maturity, and educational background of the communicant members, the general characteristics of the community, and the special needs of the believers.

I am, therefore, reluctant to make specific suggestions for fear that they will be followed! For a congregation to start an adult education effort on the basis of what worked somewhere else is wrong. They may actually end up doing some of the things other congregations do; but if they bypass an examination of their own situation, they will be using a prescription without identifying the disease. Remember that Paul did not write 1 Corinthians 13 because he thought love was a noble sentiment but because it was the only antidote for the quarreling of rival parties, their lack of respect for each other, their drunkenness and selfishness, which were described in chapters 11 and 12. Through a committee or official board, a congregation must bring to the surface the value structure which is shared by its members, and then it can make plans to discuss those values. Otherwise, congregations deal with the racial relations problem as if it were a problem only in South Africa. Or, they use their underlying competitive attitude to enhance the church's reputation in the community in every measurable item, such as size of budget, number of members, or quality of organ; these become the criteria of success. Unless the value structure itself is treated, study of the Christian tradition will be only a mental exercise or else it will be twisted to support the social values already accepted.

In some churches, it would be possible to organize a group of adults to teach themselves by having a common textbook or an agreement that a certain book of the Bible plus certain commentaries were to be used. Such groups, numbering about twenty in size, would assign to couples or small groups the sections to be studied so that each session would start with a report from these studies. There should be a leader for the discussion. Such a self-taught group could start off by selecting areas to be investigated, such as modern art and what it says for man's condition. Another group might undertake to find out what the local Jewish people thought about problems among their people. Another could seek to make connections with the nearest Catholic church and find out how the changes proposed at Vatican Council II were working out and what they thought were the major problems in Catholic-Protestant relations in that community. Other task groups could investigate the way juvenile delinquency was handled in the community or what the minority racial groups believed to be the barriers to, and possibilities for, good relations within the community. By properly scheduling these reports and by allowing six to eight weeks for discussion of each area investigated, an adult group could use a year in delving deeply into the nature of contemporary man and the human situation in which he lives.

With this basic proposition in mind, we review briefly a few other specific opportunities for adults to search the tradition for contemporary meaning. All congregations have official groups in charge of the management and various phases of the church's work. If thirty to forty minutes of the official board's meeting time could be scheduled for organized study of the Bible or for topics related to their work, the study function could become a normal part of administration without adding any extra meetings. Christian education committees could profitably study the theories of Christian education or the relation of the church to public education; or they could devise ways to test the Biblical understanding of the congregation in order to bring the church school teaching closer to the interpreted motifs which are already operating in the congregation. Perhaps we should *require* that all of our official boards budget a third of their time for study. Such a rule would dramatize the fact that individuals are agents of communication and that they must continually develop their understanding of Christianity in order to be effective as persons in the office through which they are serving.

In some congregations, short-term study groups by occupations are helpful, for there are few places where doctors, lawyers, and businessmen can gather to discuss the ethical decisions they face every day. These groups should not be allowed to solidify into permanent subunits; that would prevent a sharing of religious experience throughout the congregation, which is essential to its well-being.

There should be short-term training courses to help the laity perfect its ministry. We are counseled from the pulpit that we ought to do certain things; through church publications we are inundated with suggestions from our national boards about things we ought to be doing; and we can observe conditions in the community which the church could modify and improve, yet seldom is any guidance given as to how these things might be done. Thus, we only heighten the sense of guilt which comes from not doing what we ought to do. Our finest learning comes when we have to face situations as Christian persons, and our joy in serving comes when we do what we know how to do. These can be linked when we help people learn how to minister. Visiting the sick is an illustration. Not everyone has this ability; but there are fundamental elements in visitation, including the use of Scripture and prayer, that can be taught. A group formed on this basis should practice its ministry and report back to the larger group the experiences its members are having, discussing how the conditions thus reported are to be handled. Out of these reports will come some of the most perplexing and common human experiences such as grief, guilt, need of reassurance; all of these should be topics of study by the training group. I mention visitation because it is one of the most obvious ministries that a community of believers can maintain, and also to show how such a group can be a springboard into a study of some of the most profound religious problems.

Training groups can be formed about many areas of ministry, such as social action, community service, teaching in the church school, or tutoring public school children. But it is essential that these groups not learn a few methods of work and then be dismissed to perform this ministry on their own. It is imperative that the people involved in practicing their ministry bring back to their group in the church for discussion and further study the experiences and problems they are having. It is in this kind of study and participation that we are forced to learn and through which we formulate meaning.[11]

The congregation should give more attention to the ways (in addition to public worship) everyone can be engaged in common study in response to common themes or seasons. Perhaps Advent and Lent offer the best possibilities for a coordinated effort of study, from four to six weeks in length. Through preaching, common Bible study, plays, art exhibits, films, and ungraded discussion groups a series of topics can be studied which will enrich everyone's experience and help demonstrate that the congregation is made up of people of various ages, vocations, educational attainments, and abilities. Such occasions need to be carefully planned by a representative group so that the various parts fit the needs of the congregation, rather than being just an assemblage of programs topically arranged which people are invited to attend. If a play is enacted, it should be related to the general theme. Time should be scheduled for a thorough discussion of it in all of the church school classes or adult groups the next Sunday.

We have come this far before mentioning adult Bible study classes in order to show that congregational education can operate in a variety of ways other than formal adult classes. Classes of this nature are important and should be continued. In spite of the weakness of the traditional adult Bible class, it has been—in many congregations—the only effort toward adult education which Sunday by Sunday required adults to read the Bible and ponder its meaning. Many suggestions have been made to improve the teaching and diversify the subject matter of these classes. The main problem is to prevent their getting in a rut. When an adult class runs along the same path for a number of years, it becomes more and more the means of satisfying the social needs of the members rather than an effort to understand the Bible. In order to make the whole congregation the primary society, adult study groups should be formed and reformed annually with new combinations of teachers, adults, and curriculum.

LEADERSHIP

Leadership for faith communication in the congregation is difficult to describe because the goal of leadership is not subject to immediate verification. Some adults are able to raise their children

with an excellent combination of love and discipline yet have no conscious understanding about how they do it. Some adults are able to participate in the community of believers intelligently and creatively without being able to give a rational explanation of how they do it. Of course, we would prefer to have all of our adults be able to live and explain the faith; but we know that faith in God is independent of formal academic training.

There is no way satisfactorily to untangle faith and knowledge except to put faith first and to identify its human source, the community of believers. Anselm's definition of theology, which he adapted from a motto of Augustine, is still the best, "Faith seeking understanding." Understanding will condition a faith but will not produce it. All of this has a direct bearing on leadership in the church. To depend for leadership entirely on formal educational attainment in any field, including social science, will not guarantee a communication of faith. On the other hand, little or poor academic training may keep a person in superstition and may let him continue harmful practices or propagate inaccurate information. In their procedures for selecting ministers, denominations have never solved this problem, although they have set up procedures which eliminate the extremes and regulate to some extent the type of person who becomes a professional leader in the church. This is usually done by requiring formal, theological training which also includes supervised practical work in relation to counseling, preaching, and teaching. In addition, the denomination—through the bishop, presbytery, conference, or other agency—judges the person and his "spiritual" qualities before ordination or certification. The church has found no substitute for these procedures in achieving some balance between the three elements in leadership: (1) knowledge, (2) skill, and (3) faith qualities. We should follow these same procedures in selecting our lay leadership.

In selecting lay leadership for the church school, the congregation has most often sought the people with the faith qualities because they were already motivated to teach. We follow a sound instinct by this procedure, but we have made two mistakes. The most frequently made mistake is the assumption that if a person has faith, all other deficiencies may be overcome. Our second mistake is made when we think that with skills or knowledge we can overcome a lack of faith.

There is no easy or clear solution to this problem. It is one of our foremost problems in church work. The United Presbyterian Church, U.S.A., has just completed the most comprehensive study ever undertaken of the use of church school curriculum. That study shows the church school teachers to be behind the average layman and minister in understanding the meaning of the Bible.[12] Thus, in the heart of our most elaborate, widespread, and expensive effort to communicate faith we have a person who screens out what the best scholarship of our day says about the meaning of our faith. There is no reason to doubt that this same general condition prevails in other main-line Protestant denominations in America. But we cannot solve our problem by launching a campaign to update the Biblical knowledge of our leaders without indirectly teaching that knowledge is more important than faith.

Our best possibility for keeping all three leadership qualities in reasonable harmony and in proper relation to the mission of the church is to see leadership development as a by-product of our congregational life, especially of our adult education program. If a person actively participates in some units of the adult educational program, we can assume that some measure of faith is at work. If he is engaged in study we can see the result of his work by his comments, his questions, and his use of time. If he is interested in assuming a leadership role, he can join one of the church training groups where skills can be developed, or he can become an apprentice teacher or group leader and learn the skill from others who are practicing it. But we must not let the process end there. The leader must have opportunities to grow and to explore more fully his adult religious problems. Unless he does this, he will not be able to teach the beliefs of the church *as one who is himself a learner and believer*. This means that we should limit the terms of teachers and leaders, requiring them to join adult groups for a time before they return to teaching.

Churches that think of the communication of faith as something we must do for children and youth are forever struggling with the problem of securing teachers and leaders; the motivation is defensive, i.e., we must keep Christianity alive by teaching it to our children. This attitude is what makes congregations traditional. It is not until we think of the communication of the faith as first a responsibility of *adults to each other* that we make tradition a creative "act" of transmission that requires our best thought and mature judgment. When adults take seriously the task of interpreting the faith for themselves they are motivated to share the faith that enlivens and enriches their own life.

Thus far, we have been discussing leadership within the church and particularly within the educational work of the church, because this is the obvious need. But we must do more. The church does not exist to serve itself but the community in which it lives and the Kingdom of God in the whole world. A congregation through its worship and work can serve the needs of the world through a critical appraisal of what governments do in international relations and in the forming of national policies. Beyond this, the congregation as a group probably cannot go, although the members of the congregation may be enlightened and inspired to serve the Kingdom of God in their regular field of work.

The place where Protestantism is weak is in the church's relation to the community in which it lives. I think this is because the average American Protestant has blurred the boundary between the church and the community. For example, the first amendment to the Constitution, enacted in 1791, separated the church from the state; but the Protestant religion was taught as a regular part of the public school curriculum until the 1830's and 40's, and it was not until the time of the Civil War that the public schools were free of direct Protestant control. Many of our laws regarding the church (no taxation) or the clergy (no military service required) or Sunday (no secular work) reflect a Christianity that expected the community to enforce its world view and value system. Through their superiority in numbers in the electorate, Protestants could write the laws, the eighteenth amendment prohibiting the use of alcoholic beverages being the last major example of the Protestant effort to get the nation to enforce its will. When Protestants through the electorate did not get their laws passed, they assumed that individual leaders in places of power in business and government could deal with social issues. Now, neither of these methods of work is usable nationally, although they still operate in the South and in other sections where Protestants are in the majority. However, in the Protestant mind the attitude lingers on that we are living in a country that is "ours" in business and politics, so the church can restrict itself to the "religious" sphere. This separation of the church as an institution from secular affairs in the community has made the congregation more concerned about providing educational and social services to its members than about its responsibility for all people in the community. One of our major tasks in the future is to change this attitude.

CONGREGATIONAL CURRICULUM

The deliberate words and actions that parents and adults use in all kinds of specific events and the quality of the corporate life of the believers *are* curriculum. Although the New Testament church contained many individuals who did not live by the value system of the new religion, we can tell from Paul's letters that the inner circle of believers generated a tremendous power and formed a style of life that was in sharp contrast to the prevailing moral standards of the Romans and Greeks. Christians for several hundred years refused to serve in the Roman army. The heroism of Christianity in the face of persecution is well known. It is not my intention to idealize the New Testament church and shout a challenge to the contemporary church. It is my hope that we will see that *the process* which produced the character of early Christianity is still going on. The process is not at fault. The problem lies with what we put into the process. For example, Seventh-Day Adventists, Jehovah's Witnesses, and other sect groups are producing character that is in significant ways different from the standard American type.

The problem in main-line Protestant churches is that the process of transmitting a tradition is working too well—it is producing in the rising generation what the adults actually believe! Therefore, all attempts to reform the Protestant church that are aimed exclusively at individuals rather than at communities of believers, or that try to direct the children and youth apart from their natural socializers (the adults), or that avoid the events taking place in the community will be doomed to failure or to minor successes. There is no New Testament book addressed to individuals or to children. Philemon is about an individual, Onesimus; but the burden of the book is how the house church is to receive the runaway slave (Philemon 1).

Paul's letters are our best paradigm for congregational curricula. The Corinthian letters are an outstanding example. · Reading through the Corinthian letters will show that there are three elements in a congregational curriculum: specific events that are taking place, a larger human situation that must be taken into consideration, and the meaning of the gospel under these circumstances. Note in First Corinthians a few of the curriculum areas Paul identifies for the believers in Corinth. Chapter 3: situation— new believers (verses 1-3); event—division into followers of Paul or Apollos (verses 3-5); teaching—we are to be fellow workers and servants of Christ (verses 5-23; 4:1-21). Chapter 5: situation —immorality (verse 1a); event—case of immorality (verse 1b); teaching—remove the offender (verses 2-13). If the church did remove the offender, could there be a more powerful way to teach? Today we would probably consider Paul's judgment too harsh, as he did not seem to leave much room for rehabilitation of the offender; but if we do nothing to define membership, we are teaching that the church has no seriously held beliefs. Chapter 6: situation—how to adjudicate the difference between members; event— a law court case between members; teaching—set up an informal church court. Trace through the rest of the letter and find how Paul deals with marriage (chapter 7), gives bases for making practical ethical judgments (chapters 8 and 9), tells how to administer the Lord's Supper properly (chapter 11), shows the way people with various gifts ought to function in the church (chapter 12), tells how to relate to each other in love (chapter 13), advises concerning those who speak ecstatically (chapter 14), talks of death (chapter 15), and defines stewardship (chapter 16). We sense all through Paul's letter that although he has a clear idea about what these Christians in Corinth ought to do, the congregation's members must take responsibility for these matters and decide for themselves.

The process of communication which Paul so clearly follows is the same process with which we must work. The finest curriculum is that which is developed locally. There is no reason why a congregation cannot be more articulate about this process. Probably we cannot deal with highly specific individual moral problems with the aggressiveness that Paul did, but there are many other areas in which we can be direct. I suggested earlier in this chapter that adults can be formed into task groups to focus attention on community problems and that the normal administrative policies of the church, including the budget, should be elevated to top rank and used as the area in which we work out the meaning of our faith. Although controversy and conflict will be an inevitable feature of this approach, such a condition will assure us that we are dealing with the issues that make a difference to the people involved.

We have been insisting that curriculum is related to events which happen in the community of believers, because it is out of the handling of these things that meaning is derived. But there is another reason why the whole process has a local character. The elements that go into the process all need interpretation and judgment related to the local community. Similar events have different meanings under different circumstances. If a person steals, would this be in itself a subject of discussion in a local congregation of believers? It depends on the person and the situation. A mentally retarded child who steals small objects and an adolescent who on one occasion took a magazine from the drugstore and the adult who habitually steals from stores all present different problems.

PRINTED CURRICULUM

This foregoing approach to the communication of faith—as being centered in a community of believers—seems in principle to block all outside efforts or materials that would help guide the congregation. In some ways that is true, for the local leaders and congregation will inevitably interpret everything that impinges on their life; and they can consciously or unconsciously twist all incoming materials and messages to suit their viewpoint. But in some important ways this is not true. The church has always been more than the congregation. The New Testament rules out the absolute authority of the local congregation. Paul's letters are to local congregations, yet they are full of allusions to the church as a world-wide unity of believers. The pastoral epistles and Luke-Acts also support and enhance the idea that the church as the whole is the new Israel which has an authority and structure of its own.

These same processes go on today. The local congregation has to deal with events which happen within its fellowship and they must do so on the basis of the general truths of Christianity. Yet, at the same time, the congregation can participate with other churches to provide better teaching materials for the communication of faith. I have already pointed out that Matthew's Gospel was probably composed as a communicants' class manual; certainly the Gospels were used to train new converts in the meaning of the Christian faith; and the pastoral epistles are the first effort to regularize the church's ministry, government, and mission. Since New Testament times, the church has always written catechisms, creeds, or manuals to identify, stabilize, and propagate Christianity.

Today, this teaching function is done in denominational church school materials. One can tell more about a church's contemporary self-understanding by reading the church school materials than through the creeds or historical documents which formed the denomination. It is important for a denomination to assemble its theologians, Bible scholars, and educators every few decades to form a new curriculum and thereby to refresh its teaching ministry and itself by means of an organized sifting of its tradition in the light of current scholarship.

But a printed curriculum presents us with two problems: (1) How are we to reconcile the dynamic, congregational process that is constantly going on with the balanced, sequential printed curriculum materials which are sent to the congregation? (2) On what basis can printed curricula be devised if the congregation is the center of the process?

There must be a certain amount of ambiguity in our reply to the first question, for the two things cannot be completely reconciled. The local congregation has to meet events and contingencies as they come up or lose all touch with human life as it is lived; yet it cannot restrict its study to the local scene without losing perspective and a sense of solidarity with people of the same faith who are living elsewhere under different conditions. A tension between the two will always be present. There are two ways we can use this tension to advantage in congregational education.

First, a congregation with good leadership and ideal circumstances can produce its own printed curriculum. This seldom happens because it involves so much work, but we can imagine its possibilities. The adults of the congregation could develop a study program of the Bible and theology and make it their task to produce materials for each of the children's classes in the church school. To do so, they would have to wrestle with the meaning of faith and the mission of the whole church. Needless to say, if adults did this and also had some training in teaching they could staff the church school without further ado.

Second, a congregation under normal leadership could rewrite the denominational printed materials. Given all of the problems of the church school and the shortage of good teachers, it still would be within the range of possibility for a group of adults to slowly work through all of the materials the denomination publishes for an age level and then discuss all aspects of the material: The Biblical passages used—should others be substituted? The method of interpretation—is it Biblically sound? The activities suggested —are they appropriate? The topics selected—are they appropriate for that church? After working through all of this, making substitutions and changes, certain members of the adult group could then undertake the teaching the next year. If adult groups were properly scheduled, most of next year's teachers would be working this year with other adults preparing an adaptation of the denominational printed materials for each age level.

The second problem about a printed curriculum is the basis on which it is prepared. Originally, printed curriculum for the Sunday school was prepared to supply a logically sequential treatment of the Bible, adapted to age level understanding so that all of the Bible would be covered within a certain number of years. With the development of the religious education movement, the child and his religious situation at various age levels became the bases of printed curriculum. In recent years denominations have used a variety of curriculum designs to honor the child and his developmental level on the one hand and the church's theology on the other. However, most of these designs tend to assume that the child at different age levels has a certain mental capacity and experience which determines what is to be learned at that stage. The Bible and Christian tradition become the warehouse of things from which selections are made on the basis of the child's developmental age. This approach, regardless of the specific way it is packaged in a curriculum, assumes that the communication of faith can be made effective to the children without *necessarily* being connected with the full life of the congregation.

The issue here is not whether education is person-centered or not. All education must be person-centered. The issue is whether church education has to be oriented to the limited world of the child or whether education can be oriented to the real world of the adults, with the child at his stage of development becoming a learner of what it means to be a responsible adult Christian in his community. If it can be adult-oriented, it will have possibilities of being an "act" of tradition; that is, a reflection on the meaning of the tradition before it is transmitted.

In practical terms the proposals of the United Presbyterian Church, U.S.A., to build a new curriculum on the basis of abilities which adult Christians should have seems promising. The United Presbyterian Church has proposed five abilities that they believe adult Christians should have, and they are planning a curriculum that will at each developmental level prepare a child so that he will eventually have those abilities when he becomes a communicant member of the church. This is a radical reorientation of education. It focuses attention on adults, the persons who are deeply involved in all of the interaction in the congregation and who are the agents of communication in all three of the natural processes that are going on in the congregation. It sets performance standards and therefore moves away from the endless arguments about whether faith or knowledge, law or grace, past or present, ideal or action, should be dominant in the educational venture. By using ability goals, we transcend these ancient dichotomies and observe what adults should be able to do. These abilities can also be demonstrated, therefore religious education has criteria for judging growth and development which at the adult level have been almost nonexistent.[13]

In such a scheme, the curriculum for the children would be worked out at each developmental stage on the basis of what a person at that age level can learn and do that is interesting and necessary if he is going to have the particular ability when he is mature. The curriculum in this arrangement is always building toward definite abilities that responsible Christian adults should have. It honors the child's developmental stages by dealing with the Christian faith at different levels of awareness, but these stages are linked in progression toward an adult goal. It is also possible to test performance along the way. If we say that in late childhood (ages 10-12) a child can understand the chronology of historical events and that this is a necessary part of the ability to interpret the Bible, we could plan units of Bible study for that age level and then test the child's ability to get that part of his religious education at that appropriate time. Likewise, if myths are not well understood until early adolescence (ages 12-14), we should not go into the Genesis account for serious sequential study until that age level; but when we do, we should expect the child to grasp the meaning of this type of literature.

Although many problems will emerge in this curriculum plan, it does have the possibility of freeing the church school for instruction. Edward Farley has recently pointed out that American religious education for over half a century has confused nurture and instruction, assuming that the church school can nurture faith and planning its curriculum for that purpose. But, he says, we would be better served if we used the small amount of time available in the church school for honest instruction and let the nurture take place elsewhere.[14] His basic thesis is sound. This approach would give us a strategy whereby a church school would be more sharply defined as instruction in the Christian faith, and the fostering and living of the faith would be more consciously seen as a function of the whole congregation and of the home. A perfect illustration of the process of nurture that should surround instruction is seen in our baptismal practices in the Reformed tradition. Parents present their children for baptism and vow to bring them up "in the nurture and admonition of the Lord." Then the congregation is charged to *receive the child and promise to sponsor him,* so that he may eventually "confess Christ as his Lord and Savior."

The role of the family in religious education has been reassessed several times in the past century. Horace Bushnell, concerned about a revivalism which insisted on conversion at adolescence and a religious education in the church school which prepared children for it, wrote of the role of the family in socializing the child in the ways of faith long before this process was studied by social scientists. Bushnell's book *Christian Nurture* continues to be helpful because he so carefully observed and described the natural process by which a child absorbs the faith of the family.[15]

Religious educators have generally honored the home for its power to form the child, but in the last quarter of a century two tendencies have emerged that must be corrected. One tendency is to idealize the family in terms of its tremendous power for shaping personality and to build an educational strategy on the basis of what the church can get the family to teach in the home. The basic weakness of this emphasis is the assumption that parents are Christian and that they have skills to teach in the home. What actually happens in this strategy is a legitimizing of whatever values, world view, and self-image the parents happen to have. Rather than turning religious education over to the parents exclusively, we must recognize that the parents are also under judgment and need their Christian understanding expanded and clarified while they fulfill their role as parents. Therefore, we must give first attention to the continual training of adults who are parents, so that they may grow "in grace and knowledge" and then, as part of their training, help them better to perform their role as parents and teachers in the home. But whatever we do with parents, we should do on the assumption that the home is a home and not a little church.

The other tendency is to depreciate the home. Religious educators who take this position look at the high divorce rate, the large number of working mothers, the early independence of adolescents, the materialistic attitude of parents, and say that we can make little or no effort to do religious education in the home. Rather, they say, we must depend upon the church school, the congregration, or some other social group to do what the home is no longer able to do. Sometimes advocates of this point of view advance the notion that society is changing so rapidly that the home cannot possibly add anything but confusion to an already bad situation.

These critical strictures on the home contain some truth. In certain congregations they determine the method of work. Letty Russell, minister of a church in the East Harlem Protestant Parish, has written a description of the home situation in her congregation which precludes the use of the home as an agent for religious education; under these circumstances I am sure she is right in seeking other ways and other agencies for religious education.[16]

In other congregations we must make a different appraisal of the family situation. It may be that many of the critical strictures apply and we should be cautious about any strategy that uses the family for religious education. However, we must also constantly remind ourselves that children are born into families, that they are raised in families (or some substitute small social group), and that such a group will function to give the child his values and self-image. Therefore, we must not idealize or ignore this powerful process of nurture. We must help the adults learn how they can function as Christian parents in the home.

A NEW DELIBERATENESS

The question could be asked, "Is it possible for the average congregation to follow this approach to communication?" There are two answers. First, insofar as this approach is an accurate description of the process of communication of any faith held by any stable group of people, it is a description of how the Christian faith of a congregation is communicated among its members and to the children. In that sense, the average congregation is inevitably communicating whatever faith it has. But what the questioner usually has in mind in such a question is whether it is possible in the average congregation to change the world view, value system, or self-image that is being communicated. This is indeed a problem.

I would not want to underestimate the apathy, conformity, or downright hostility to change which lies beneath the surface of the average congregation.[17] To make changes requires constant pressure and persistence in changing church policies over a long period of time and through a variety of channels. This approach through the adults is slow. But gains, once made, are rather certain to remain, and the possibilities of adults becoming more articulate and influential in all other relationships in the community is good. Changes can come if the leaders—lay or clerical—will begin to be more deliberate about all of the activities in which the congregation is engaged, ferreting out and critically appraising the presuppositions on which the members pattern their life and using the instructional periods for serious study and reflection about the nature and the meaning of the Christian tradition.

The pressure against change is so great in most congregations that we cannot assume that significant changes can be made in a reasonable length of time. Other ways must also be found to make the mission of the church more effective. One of these other methods is to establish congregations on the basis of a clearly defined covenant of membership which functions properly from the outset. Such congregations could start out to actualize the ministry of Christ by having its members take vows to each other—pledging their time for study as well as their money for the enterprise, outlining practical duties of ministry to each other, and providing ways of exploring and exercising their ministry in the community. Such a deliberate congregation should also set itself clearly against expenditures for costly buildings, competitive programs, or any other manifestation of the American success motif. A few such congregations could be the leaven that would permeate the traditional, institutionalized church and reclaim it for Christ and his redemptive work in the world.

Notes and Acknowledgments

I. CONCEPTIONS OF COMMUNICATION

1. When the empirical social scientist does research in areas which might be helpful to us, his work has limited value because of his research model. The model is like this: Two groups of children will be matched by all of the measurable factors such as age, race, sex, and IQ. One group, the "control" group, will follow their normal activities, while some change will be made in the second "experimental" group, such as a new teaching method. Later both groups will be tested. If the experimental group shows improved behavior, it is assumed that the one change in teaching method caused the change in performance. Because they are getting attention that the control group is not getting, the experimental group will often work harder or will change its behavior to conform to the expectation of the experiment. However, this distortion known as the "Hawthorne effect" is not my point here. Rather, I am suggesting that the model itself has limitations when applied to the religious life. Can we be sure that all of the variables which are supposed to be held constant between the control group and the experimental group are held constant? Can we be sure that the persons involved in both the control and experimental groups are not changing deep within themselves without this change being registered on the measuring instruments? I believe the answer to both of these questions is no.

There are many variables in human conduct that are not subject to precise measurement, such as the strength of love and hate, the amount of fear that a person has, or, more important, an individual's deference to authority or his ego strength in relation to his peers. All of these elements are involved in human conduct (particularly in group experiments) as well as are facts such as age, race, sex, and IQ. Also, the sources of motivation, deep within a person, may be changing without the person's conscious awareness of the change. To make generalizations about human behavior on the basis of judgments about, or measurements of, conduct that appears on the surface at the time an experiment is conducted is to ignore the power and direction of changes that are taking place deep within the unconscious levels of our lives. For example, a high school student can be judged by teachers and tests to be well-adjusted and most likely to succeed; ten years later this person may be still struggling with deep inner tensions which were in his life all the time but which are now coming into his conscious mind.

An excellent illustration of this point is found in Percival M. Symonds, *Adolescent Fantasy* (New York: Columbia University Press, 1949). In this book Symonds gives full details on the case of Jack and Jimmy. Thirteen years later he repeated the study with the same people, and neither Jack nor Jimmy had developed exactly as expected. The follow-up study is found in Percival M. Symonds and Arthur R. Jensen, *From Adolescent to Adult* (New York: Columbia University Press, 1961).

2. The word "sentiment" is now being used by social scientists as the best word for the "relatively stable and recurrent compounds of thought, feeling, and striving which relate a person to the objects in his environment. They are the emotionally-toned 'templates' through which he defines 'what is,' 'what ought to be,' and 'what is desirable.' " It is in this sense that the word is used in this book. See Alexander H. Leighton, *My Name Is Legion* (New York: Basic Books, Inc., 1959), p. 396 and pp. 226-275.

II. THE FORMATIVE POWER OF CULTURE

1. Talcott Parsons and Edward A. Shils, eds., *Toward a General Theory of Action* (Cambridge: Harvard University Press, 1954), pp. 1-27.

2. Ralph Linton, *The Cultural Background of Personality* (New York: D. Appleton-Century Company, Inc., 1945), p. 19.

3. *Ibid.*, p. 32.

4. Charles Winick, *Dictionary of Anthropology* (New York: Philosophical Library, 1956), p. 144.

5. Jurgen Ruesch, "Sociocultural and Personality System," in Roy R. Grinker, *Toward a Unified Theory of Human Behavior* (New York: Basic Books, Inc., 1958), p. 328.

6. Linton, *op. cit.*, pp. 25-26. The notions I have been discussing about primacy of culture came from Linton, although I have adapted his points to the purpose of this study.

7. C. Ellis Nelson, "Innovations for the Educational Mission of the Church" (New York: National Council of Churches, 1965).

8. Dorothy Lee, *Freedom and Culture* (Englewood Cliffs, N.J.: Prentice-Hall, 1959), p. 164.

9. Robert Redfield, "The Primitive World View," *Proceedings of the American Philosophical Society*, 96:30-36 (1952), p. 30. See also Robert Redfield, *The Primitive World and Its Transformations* (Ithaca: Cornell University Press, 1953), Chapter IV.

10. Leslie A. White, "The World of the Keresan Pueblo Indians," Stanley Diamond, ed., *Primitive Views of the World* (New York: Columbia University Press, 1960), p. 84.

11. Erik H. Erikson, *Identity and the Life Cycle* (New York: International Universities Press, Inc., 1959), pp. 21-22.

12. Kenneth W. Morgan, "Buddhists in Saigon," *The Christian Century*, January 26, 1966, p. 108.

13. Erikson, *op. cit.*, p. 157.

14. *Ibid.*, p. 158.

15. Parsons and Shils, *op. cit.*, p. 395. The comments that follow this definition come from the same source.

16. *Ibid.*, p. 396.

17. United States Statutes at Large, 87th Congress, 1961 (Volume 75), Public Law 87-195, p. 424.

18. Parsons and Shils, *op. cit.*, p. 398.

19. *Ibid.*, p. 400.

20. Ralph H. Gabriel, *Traditional Values in American Life* (New York: Harcourt, Brace and Company, 1960). This essay was prepared for the U.S. National Commission for UNESCO. The Harcourt, Brace edition is in their "Teacher's Notebook in the Social Studies" series, Fall, 1960, and has no page numbers. Excerpts are used by permission of the publisher.

If the reader wants to get a better grasp of how cultural values shape a style of life, he could start with Margaret Mead, ed., *Cultural Patterns and Technical Change* (New York: The New American Library of World Literature, Inc., 1955), or Edward T. Hall, *The Silent Language* (New York: Doubleday and Company, 1959). W. Lloyd Warner's *American Life: Dream and Reality* (Chicago: University of Chicago Press, 1957) is an effort to interpret American values to Englishmen.

An excellent treatment of cultural values in relation to communication is Jurgen Ruesch and Gregory Bateson, *Communication* (New York: W. W. Norton Company, 1951). Comparisons are made between American and European cultures, and special attention is given to many ordinary behavior patterns and the place of morals in American values.

21. H. Richard Niebuhr, *The Social Sources of Denominationalism* (New York: The World Publishing Company, 1962; originally published in 1929).

22. Eugene A. Nida, *Customs, Culture, and Christianity* (London: The Tyndale Press, 1963), p. 198. See also Nida's *God's Word in Man's Language* (1952) and *Message and Mission* (1960) published by Harper & Row, New York.

23. Clyde Kluckhohn, *Navaho Witchcraft*, abridged from Part II, Section 3, by J. Milton Yinger in *Religion, Society and the Individual* (New York: The Macmillan Company, 1957), pp. 359-360.

24. Gordon W. Allport and Leo F. Postman, "The Basic Psychology of Rumor," Guy E. Swanson and others, *Readings in Social Psychology* (New York: Henry Holt and Company, rev. ed., 1952), p. 163.

25. Harry Stack Sullivan, *The Interpersonal Theory of Psychiatry* (New York: W. W. Norton and Company, Inc., 1953), pp. 170, 319-320, 374. See also Carl R. Rogers, *On Becoming a Person* (Boston: Houghton Mifflin Company, 1961), p. 115.

26. C. Ellis Nelson, "The Christian Education of Conscience," *The Princeton Seminary Bulletin,* September, 1961. This article was written before Vatican Council II and cites a standard Roman Catholic textbook on conscience. That citation is no longer appropriate, as moral theology in Roman Catholicism is not now restricted to a church-centered conscience.

27. Bruno Bettelheim was able to keep his sanity and his life while in a German concentration camp because he could refer mentally to his historical Jewish identity. See Erikson, *op. cit.*, p. 27, note 6.

28. Linton, *op. cit.*, pp. 100-101.

29. Allison Davis, and others, *Deep South: A Social Anthropological Study of Caste and Class* (Chicago: The University of Chicago Press, 1941; abridged ed., 1965). See also W. Lloyd Warner and others, *Color and Human Nature: Negro Personality Development in a Northern City* (Washington, D.C.: American Council on Education, 1941).

30. Edgar Z. Friedenberg, *The Vanishing Adolescent* (New York: Dell Publishing Company, Inc., 1962), pp. 116-117.

III. THE DYNAMICS OF RELIGIOUS TRADITION

1. Gerhard Ebeling, *Word and Faith* (Philadelphia: Fortress Press, 1963), p. 363.

2. *Ibid.,* p. 364.

3. Albert C. Outler, "Traditions in Transit," in World Council of Churches Commission on Faith and Order, *The Old and the New in the Church* (Minneapolis: Augsburg Publishing House, 1961), p. 44.

4. The book of Revelation pictures the church on the battlefield of history. Not all churches are faithful to God, but the image one gets in this book is that "time will tell" and the present duty is to be loyal to God.

5. Eusebius, *The History of the Church from Christ to Constantine,* G. A. Williamson, tr. (Middlesex, England: Penguin Books, 1965), III: 39, p. 150.

6. Irenaeus, Bishop of Lyons, "The Refutation and Overthrow of the Knowledge Falsely So Called," Book III, Cyril C. Richardson, ed., *Early Christian Fathers* (London: SCM Press Ltd., 1953), Vol. I, p. 371.

7. *Ibid.,* p. 373.

8. *Ibid.,* p. 370.

9. Gerhard von Rad, *Genesis,* John H. Marks, tr. (Philadelphia: The Westminster Press, 1961), pp. 43-83.

10. The Mishnah is an effort to preserve and apply the law that developed over a period of about four hundred years. In this sense the Mishnah is the notebook of Jewish thinkers who were self-conscious about their responsibility to interpret the tradition as they passed it on. For a taste of this work, see *Pirke Aboth* ("Chapters of the Fathers") in Herbert Danby, ed. and tr., *The Mishnah* (Oxford: The Clarendon Press, 1933), pp. 446-461.

11. W. C. van Unnik, "Luke-Acts, a Storm Center in Contemporary Scholarship," Leander E. Keck and J. Louis Martyn, eds., *Studies in Luke-Acts* (New York: Abingdon Press, 1966), pp. 24-25.

12. James Barr in *Old and New in Interpretation* (London: SCM Press Ltd., 1966) makes the point in several places that there is no stage of development in the Bible where God is not known, that in Israel God is always presupposed, that tradition is always there and is used as the context for further disclosures from God. See p. 89.

13. Scholars are not agreed on the relation between Paul's writings

and the account of Paul in Acts. Apparently, what we have in Acts is Luke's interpretation of Paul or the way the church began to remember its history a generation after Paul's death. Since we are concerned about the way the church used tradition, we will cite the material from Acts. See Philipp Vielhauer, "On the 'Paulinism' of Acts," in Keck and Martyn, *op. cit.,* pp. 33-49. For a discussion that assumes Paul's speeches in Acts are reasonably correct, see C.F.D. Moule's "The Christology of Acts" in the same book, p. 173.

14. See Romans 7 for an illustration of how Paul had to work through his "law" tradition to understand Christ.

15. The Westminster Shorter Catechism, Question 4.

IV. FAITH AND SELF-IDENTIFICATION

1. Paul S. Minear, *Images of the Church in the New Testament* (Philadelphia: The Westminster Press, 1960). See also Eduard Schweizer, *Church Order in the New Testament* (London: SCM Press Ltd., 1961).

2. Paul S. Minear, "Idea of Church," in *The Interpreter's Dictionary of the Bible* (New York: Abingdon Press, 1962), Vol. A-D, p. 607.

3. *Ibid.,* p. 609.

4. Claude Welch, *The Reality of the Church* (New York: Charles Scribner's Sons, 1958), p. 165.

5. Gibson Winter, *The New Creation as Metropolis* (New York: The Macmillan Company, 1963), Chapter 1.

6. Colin W. Williams, *Where in the World?* (New York: National Council of Churches, 1963). A vast literature is developing under the general topic "renewal of the church" and it is not easy to characterize this movement. I find myself in agreement with much of the criticism of the church as being too concerned for respectability, too self-centered, and too prone to build up its institutional strength and wealth. I have no difficulty with those who want to "restructure" the church, although those who talk this way have not yet given us new structures to observe. My basic disagreement is only with those who are unwilling to live by the tradition while they re-evaluate it, or who forget the communal substructure of the church in their "busyness" to rebuild the superstructure.

7. Williams, *op. cit.,* p. 75.

8. An exception to this general statement is the book of Galatians. In Galatians Paul does become personal about his religious experiences

(1:11—2:21). But even here Paul tells his story to show God's guidance, rather than to say that others should have his experience. Then, when he begins to explain the gospel to them, he does so on the basis of God's great design, starting with Abraham (3:6—4:31).

9. R.P.C. Hanson in *Tradition in the Early Church* (London: SCM Press Ltd., 1962) points out in his chapter on "The Creed" that the church from "the earliest moment of its existence was a teaching church." We often forget the centrality of searching and teaching in the church because we tend to equate the word "church" with a doctrine of the church rather than with a community that is trying to understand and communicate its faith.

10. Although this review is in my own words, the idea came from C.F.D. Moule, *The Birth of the New Testament* (New York: Harper & Row, 1962), p. 53.

11. Krister Stendahl, *The School of St. Matthew* (Lund: C.W.K. Gleerup, 1954), pp. 20-35.

12. Moule, *op. cit.,* p. 80.

V. FAITH AND PERCEPTION

1. Eduard Schweizer, "Orthodox Proclamation" in *Interpretation,* Vol. VIII, No. 4, October 1954, pp. 387-403.

2. Edwyn Clement Hoskyns, *The Fourth Gospel* (London: Faber and Faber Ltd., 1947), Vol. 1, p. 120.

3. Schweizer, *op. cit.,* p. 402.

4. M. C. D'Arcy, S. J., *The Sense of History: Secular and Sacred* (London: Faber and Faber Ltd., 1959), pp. 60-61.

5. Thomas Jefferson, *The Life and Morals of Jesus of Nazareth* (New York: N. D. Thompson Publishing Company, 1902). Since Jefferson prepared this work as curriculum material for use by the Indians, we must list him as one of the early religious educators!

6. Rudolf Bultmann, "The Significance of the Old Testament for the Christian Faith," in Bernhard W. Anderson, ed., *The Old Testament and Christian Faith* (New York: Harper & Row, 1963), pp. 8-35.

7. Adolf Harnack, *What Is Christianity?* (New York: G. P. Putnam's Sons, 1901), pp. 321, 295, 1-20, and *passim.*

8. John Calvin, *Institutes of the Christian Religion,* John T. McNeill, ed. (London: SCM Press Ltd., 1960; Philadelphia: The Westminster Press, 1960), Vol. II, pp. 1168-1169 (IV-9-4, 5).

9. Minutes of the Seventy-Eighth General Assembly of the Presbyterian Church in the United States, 1938, p. 132.

10. Reinhold Niebuhr, *The Nature and Destiny of Man* (New York: Charles Scribner's Sons, 1949), Vol. II, pp. 1-34.

11. A. N. Whitehead, *Science and the Modern World* (Cambridge: Cambridge University Press, 1953), p. 26.

12. Herbert Butterfield, *Christianity and History* (New York: Charles Scribner's Sons, 1950), p. 110.

13. Joseph Fletcher, "Love Is the Only Measure," Part I of "The New Morality" in *Commonweal*, Vol. LXXXIII, No. 14, January 14, 1966. See also Joseph Fletcher, *Situation Ethics: The New Morality* (Philadelphia: The Westminster Press, 1966). On the other side, see James M. Gustafson, "Context Versus Principles—A Misplaced Debate in Christian Ethics," in *Harvard Theological Review*, April, 1965, pp. 171-202. See also Paul Ramsey, "Deeds and Rules in Christian Ethics," *Scottish Journal of Theology*, Occasional Papers No. 11 (Edinburgh: Oliver & Boyd Ltd., 1965).

VI. FAITH AND VALUES

1. Ernest Wright, "History and Reality," in Bernhard W. Anderson, ed., *The Old Testament and Christian Faith* (New York: Harper & Row, Publishers, 1963; copyright © Bernhard W. Anderson), p. 186. Used by permission.

2. In a book for teen-agers on morality, I attempted to interpret the Ten Commandments in relation to the Exodus experience and the teachings of Jesus. See C. Ellis Nelson, *Love and the Law* (Richmond: John Knox Press, 1963).

3. Ernest Wright, *op. cit.*, pp. 186-187.

4. John Calvin, *Institutes of the Christian Religion*, John T. McNeill, ed. (London: SCM Press Ltd., 1960; Philadelphia: The Westminster Press, 1960), Vol. 1, p. 462 (II-11-13), p. 504 (II-16-2); see also p. 162 (1-14-3).

5. C.F.D. Moule, *The Birth of the New Testament* (New York: Harper & Row, 1962), p. 68. See also pp. 68-70.

6. *Ibid.*, pp. 58-59.

7. These two illustrations are samples of many quoted by E. Earle Ellis, *Paul's Use of the Old Testament* (Edinburgh: Oliver & Boyd Ltd., 1957), p. 74. (The Isaiah reference has been changed to give the correct chapter number.)

8. C. M. Dodd, *History and the Gospel* (London: Hodder and Stoughton, rev. ed., 1964), p. 43.

9. Moule, *op. cit.*, p. 81.

10. The reader is reminded that I am using Acts because it represents the way the New Testament church first started to use tradition. See note 13 of Chapter III.

11. C. H. Dodd, *According to the Scriptures* (New York: Charles Scribner's Sons, 1953), p. 18.

12. *Ibid.*, pp. 102-103.

13. Ernest Wright, *op. cit.*, pp. 192-193.

14. *Ibid.*, p. 193.

15. Joachim Jeremias, *The Parables of Jesus* (New York: Charles Scribner's Sons, rev. ed., tr. by S. H. Hooke from the German *Die Gleichnisse Jesu*, 6th ed., 1962. Copyright 1963 SCM Press Ltd.), pp. 96-114.

VII. GUIDELINES FOR COMMUNICATING FAITH

1. William Bean Kennedy, *The Shaping of Protestant Education* (New York: Association Press, 1966).

2. An excellent survey of the Biblical view of human solidarity is by Russell Philip Shedd, *Man in Community* (London: The Epworth Press, 1958; Grand Rapids, Mich.: Wm. B. Eerdmans, 1963).

3. R. A. McGonigal, Chaplain, U.S. Navy, first called this situation to my attention by his careful study of learning theory applied to adult education.

4. A few years ago I worked out a "Criteria for Judging the Quality of Christian Education for Adults" for a workshop on adult education held at the University of Pittsburgh. This series of twenty questions probes the nature and function of the church in a practical way for the average congregation. A group of adults could take these questions as a place to start and spend a few months working out their own standards. See Lawrence C. Little, ed., *Wider Horizons in Christian Adult Education* (Pittsburgh: University of Pittsburgh Press, 1962), pp. 257-277.

5. George W. Webber, *The Congregation in Mission* (New York: Abingdon Press, 1964), pp. 74-91.

6. For a wide variety of practical suggestions from a minister, see David J. Ernsberger, *Education for Renewal* (Philadelphia: The Westminster Press, 1965).

7. Langdon Gilkey, *How the Church Can Minister to the World Without Losing Itself* (New York: Harper & Row, 1964), pp. 97-98.

8. I am using the word "strategy" here in terms of educational

policy. This use of the term and also its wider application to the church in relation to the state in education during the last seventy-five years is developed by Robert W. Lynn, *Protestant Strategies in Education* (New York: Association Press, 1964).

9. The first comprehensive and scientific study of belief systems of youth was done by Lutheran Youth Research. Five belief systems were found by cluster analysis, and these were shown to have a high positive correlation with the beliefs of the adults in the congregation. Merton P. Strommen, *Profiles of Church Youth* (St. Louis: Concordia Publishing House, 1963). See page 60 and the summary sentence, "Youth simply reflect what adult leaders in their congregations believe."

10. This brief listing of problems is not complete. Before a person launches a congregational study program, he must become familiar with the general problems of adult education. A fuller treatment of these problems and a few references to educational literature will be found in my article, "Toward Better Methods of Communicating the Christian Faith," in Lawrence C. Little, ed., *The Future Course of Christian Adult Education* (Pittsburgh: University of Pittsburgh Press, 1959), pp. 202-218.

11. J. Claude Evans, "Renewal in the Local Church," in *The Christian Century,* Vol. LXXXII, No. 47, November 24, 1965, pp. 1443-1447.

12. Jack A. Worthington, "Prospects for a 'New' Church Education," in *Religious Education,* Vol. LXI, No. 3, May-June, 1966, p. 183. The findings from this important study have not yet been published. Materials from "The United Presbyterian National Educational Survey" as they are ready are placed in the libraries of the Presbyterian seminaries and colleges and can be consulted there.

13. *Ibid.,* pp. 183-188.

14. Edward Farley, "Does Christian Education Need the Holy Spirit?": Part I, "The Strange History of Christian *Paideia,*" in *Religious Education,* Vol. LX, No. 5, September-October, 1965, pp. 339-346, and Part II, "The Work of the Spirit in Christian Education," Vol. LX, No. 6, November-December, 1965, pp. 427-436, 479. There has been considerable controversy among religious educators about these articles, and a number of replies have appeared in *Religious Education* during 1966. A careful reading of the follow-up articles will indicate that Farley was not trying to present a total theory of church education. His main contention—that religious educators generally have assumed they could do most of the necessary nurturing and

instruction in the church school through planned curriculum and directed activities—is correct.

15. Horace Bushnell, *Christian Nurture* (New Haven: Yale University Press, 1947; originally published in 1861). On page 4 he states his thesis: "That the child is to grow up a Christian, and never know himself as being otherwise."

16. Letty M. Russell, "The Family and Christian Education in Modern Urban Society," in *Union Seminary Quarterly Review*, Vol. XVI, No. 1, November, 1960, pp. 33-43.

17. George Harvey Crowell, *American Cultural Values Obstructing Christian Social Action*, Th.D. dissertation (New York: Union Theological Seminary, 1966).

Index of Scripture Passages

Index of Subjects and Names